Desert Wildflowers

Drylands of North America

Desert
Wildflowers
Drylands of North America

A Guide to Selected Wildflowers and Flowering Shrubs
from the Drylands of North America

by
David Winegar

Introduction and Illustrations
by
Earl Rosenwinkel

First Printing April, 1982
Published by Beautiful America Publishing Company
P.O. Box 608, Beaverton, Oregon 97075
Robert D. Shangle, Publisher

Library of Congress Cataloging in Publication Data
Winegar, David.
Desert Wildflowers, Drylands of North America
Includes index.
1. Desert flora — North America — Identification.
2. Wild flowers — North America — Identification.
I. Rosenwinkel, Earl.   II. Title.
QK112.W55   582.13'097   82-4340
ISBN 0-89802-371-8   AACR2

Contents

Area Covered

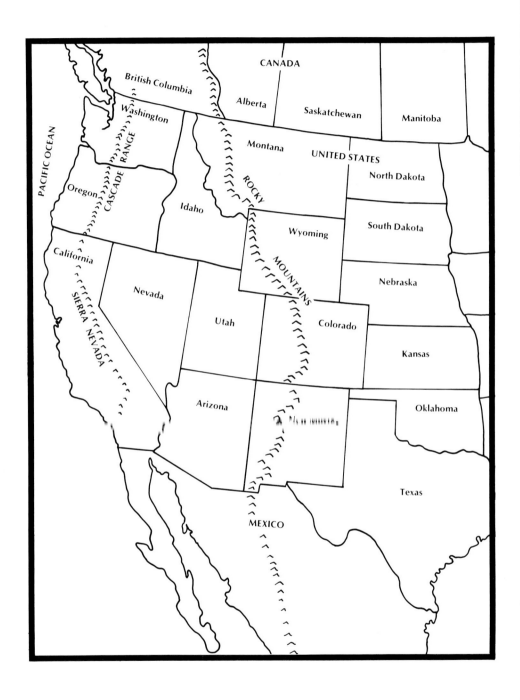

Foreword

In the spring of 1973, David Winegar came to me for assistance in a flower-photography project. This book is the outgrowth and culmination of his subsequent inspiration, hard work, note-taking, and photography during that spring, many weekends, and the summer of 1974. This book is also the result of personal struggle and sacrifice. David died November 17, 1974, in a car accident on a snowy road on Mt. Hood, while on his way back home from his last field trip. Ever since, his mother has been persistently devoted to the completion of this book, which David envisioned and did much to create.

This book is meant to be an introduction, not only to "flowers" as such, but to common, important, or interesting plant species, their place in nature, and their uses. More complete and detailed books are available in bookstores or libraries for further studies and identification.

It is my most earnest wish that this book is true to David's vision of it, and that it leads many people to a deeper understanding and love of the plant life of the drylands of North America.

Earl R. Rosenwinkel

Introduction

This book is a field guide for those who want to begin to deepen their enjoyment and understanding of the natural history of the grasslands and juniper savannas of the drier parts of North America, but who are not acquainted with the plant organs and scientific terminology needed to identify plants accurately. Although most of the plants in this book have interesting or noticeable flowers, some do not. The latter were included because they are useful to people, or are widespread in, characteristic of, or ecologically important in the area. Fortunately, these plants are easily identifiable. Even so, many plants are not included; there are far too many to fit in a field guide that is to fit into a pocket or pack.

Scientific names derived from Latin or Greek terms are the most consistently and widely used plant names, and that's why they are here in addition to the more common, or familiar, names. Also, names of plant families and descriptions of some important or interesting families are found with a descriptive picture. This classification helps in keeping the diversity of plant species in mind, and in indentifying new ones. For example—did you know that the umbel arrangement of flowers and seeds of bisquit root is the same as all other plants in the *Umbelliferae* family, such as dill, caraway, fennel, poison hemlock, and carrot? (Look up "umbel" in the Illustrations of Flower Parts and Terms!).

To identify a plant you see in the field, decide whether it is a woody plant like a tree, shrub, or vine, or whether it is more like an herb. Now like all classification schemes, even scientific ones, there are exceptions and drawbacks to this one, but one hopes you'll soon learn to tell Juniper tree seedlings from herbs! If the plant fits in the herb section, then decide whether the flower parts of the plant are in threes or sixes, as in the lily, tulip, or daffodil. If not, see whether the flower is radially symmetrical like those of the rose, cherry, and lily family flowers, or whether they are bilaterally symmetrical like orchids, peas, or beans; that is, like your body, with a left and a right side. Also at this time check to see if the flower is really a close cluster (head) of smaller flowers (florets) borne on a common base (receptacle) as in the *Compositae* family, which includes the sunflower, daisy, chrysanthemum, and dandelion. If the flowers don't have these characteristics, but they are radially symmetrical, decide what subsection they fall into according to the flower color. Many species have some variety in their flower colors, so the color subsections are broadly defined. The section or subsection you finally chose should be followed by looking at the not-too-many pictures in that section or subsection, to see which matches the plant you are interested in. Then using the Glossary and the Illustrations of Flower Parts and Terms, see if the written description of that plant also describes the one you are looking at. Also, check the flowering season, but be aware that there is variation in times of flowering, as well as in other characteristics because of differences in individual plants, in environmental factors specific to the particular site where your plant is growing, and in yearly weather.

Finally, don't be discouraged by any unsuccessful attempts! Be encouraged by the plants that you do identify and learn, and the more you learn, the easier it gets!

Earl R. Rosenwinkel

Glossary

acaulescent—without a stem.

achene—a small, dry, one-seeded fruit that does not open at maturity.

acuminate—gradually tapering to the tip. (Fig. 29).

acute—more abruptly tapering to the tip. (Fig. 30).

alternate—only one at a node. (Fig. 7).

annual—life-cycle complete in one year.

anthers—pollen-bearing part of stamen. (Fig 39d, 40d, 51d).

areoles—small, clearly marked area.

auriculate—with auricles, small lobes or appendages at base. (Fig. 34).

banner—upper enlarged petal of papilionaceous (butterfly shaped) flower. (Fig. 45f).

bidentate—two tooth-like prolongations.

biennial—life-cycle completed in two years.

bilabiate—two lipped, as in the corolla (petals) of legumes. (Fig. 44f).

bipinnate—twice pinnate, segmented segments arranged on a mid-rib. (Fig. 5).

biternate—three divisions, each of which is divided into three parts.

bracts—modified leaf, usually small, and below the flower or flower-cluster with which it is associated. (Fig. 52-57).

bulb—a shortened underground stem, hidden by and bearing leaves thickened with stored food, like onion. (Fig. 38).

calyx—all of the outermost leaves (sepals) of flower. (Fig. 39g, 40g, 46g).

campanulate—bell-shaped flower. (Fig. 41).

canescent—pale or grayish, due to growth of fine whitish hairs.

capitate—head-like, dense clusters of flowers. (Fig. 54).

capsule—a dry fruit that opens along 2 or more lines to release the seeds. (Fig. 60).

cauline—on stem above a base.

ciliate—with fringe of marginal hairs.

circinate—coiled from tip downward, with apex as center.

composite—the inflorescence (heads) of the *Compositae* family. (Fig. 47).

compound—formed by union of like parts (pistil Fig. 39c), or made up of segments (leaf Fig. 2-5).

connate—grown together from beginning of development.

cordate—heart shaped, notch at base. (Fig. 27).

corms—short, thickened underground stem with roots below, leaves above. (Fig. 37).

corolla—collectively—all the petals of a flower. (Fig. 39-48f).

corymbiform—having forms of corymb, a flower cluster in which lower and outer flowers open first with outer pedicels longer. (Fig. 55).

crenate—with rounded teeth, scalloped. (Fig. 15).

crenulate—finely scalloped.

cuneate—wedge-shaped, narrow end at base. (Fig. 33).

cyme—first flower to develop is on end, others arise below it. (Fig. 53).

deciduous—becomes detached after completion of normal function.

decumbent—base of stem resting on ground, rest turned upward.

deltoid—triangular, attached at center of base.

dentate—spreading, pointed teeth on margin. (Fig. 13).

denticulate—finely dentate.

dioecious—producing male and female flowers on separate plants.

discoid—resembles disk, with flower's head all tubular and perfect. (Fig. 46 & 47).

dissected—deeply and often repeatedly divided into small parts. (Fig. 12).

drupe—pulpy, usually one-seeded fruit, with seed enclosed by stone or pit, like a cherry or peach. (Fig. 58).

elliptic—two or three times as long as wide, uniform curvature to sides. (Fig. 22).

entire—margin not toothed or cut. (Fig. 16).

epigynous—perianth and stamens attached to top of (inferior) ovary. (Fig. 40 & 46).

falcate—curved like blade of sickle.

flabellate—fan-shaped.

fleshy—thick and juicy.

flower—part of plant containing stamens, pistil, and often sepals and petals, all borne on a receptacle. (Fig. 39).

-foliolate—suffix indicating number of leaflets.

follicle—dry fruit of one carpel (innermost leaves) opening on one line only. (Fig. 63).

fornices—set of small scales or appendages in throat corolla of some plants.

funnelform—flower (corolla) widened upward like funnel. (Fig. 42).

gametopetalous—with petals all in one piece. (Fig. 41-48).

gametosepalous—with sepals all in one piece. (Fig. 40, 44, 45g).

glabrous—smooth, without hairs.

glandular—having protuberance, appendage, or depression which produces sticky or greasy viscous substance.

globose—spherical, more or less.

gynophore—central stalk bearing collectively all carpels of flower.

helicord—apparent main axis curved in a helix, more or less.

herbaceous—with little woody tissue.

hirsute—clothed with stiff hair.

hoary—densely covered with whitish hairs.

hypanthium—ring or cup around ovary, that part of apparent calyx tube below attachment of petals.

hypogynous—flower parts borne on a receptacle, below the (superior) ovary. (Fig. 39).

inflorescence—flower-cluster or arrangement of flowers on axis. (Fig. 47, 49, 50, 51-57).

involucre—one or more whorls or crowded series of bracts below flower-cluster.

irregular—bilateral, or 2-sided (left and right) symmetry, as in flowers. (Fig. 44 & 45).

keel—prominent longitudinal ridge.

lanceolate—leaf shape, much longer than wide, tapering to both ends. (Fig. 18).

ligulate—having ligules, term applied to flattened part of the ray corolla in *Compositae* (Fig. 47f & 48f) and to appendage on upper side of leaf at junction of blade and sheath in *Gramineae* and *Cyperaceae*.

linear—long and narrow, line shaped. (Fig. 24).

lobed—large indentations or teeth. (Fig. 10 & 11).

lyrate-pinnatifid—terminal segment much larger than others.

-merous—suffix referring to parts in each circle of floral organs.

mucilaginous—slimy or viscid, resembling muscilage.

obcordate—like cordate, but notch at tip. (Fig. 28).

oblanceolate — inversely lanceolate, broadest above middle, tapers to base. (Fig. 19).

oblong — leaf form, length greater than width, sides parallel most of length (Fig. 23).

obovate — like ovate, but larger at distal end. (Fig. 20).

obtuse — blunt. (Fig. 31).

ochroleucous — yellowish-white.

opposite (leaves) — two structures (leaves) at a place on the stem. (Fig. 8).

orbicular — circular in form. (Fig. 25).

ovary — expanded basal part of carpel or pistil, contains ovules (undeveloped seeds). (Fig. 39c & 51c).

ovate — egg shaped, larger end toward base. (Fig. 17).

palmate — more than three parts radiating from common point. (Fig. 3 & 11).

panicle — flower-cluster (inflorescence) where primary axis branches into secondary, etc. (Fig. 56).

papilionaceous — resembling butterfly, applied to usual form of flower in Pea family. (Fig. 45).

pappus — hairs, scales, and/or bristles composing modified calyx of *Compositae*. (Fig. 46g).

pedicel — stalk or stem of individual flower. (Fig. 39, 40, 44, 45, 52, 57i).

peduncle — base of inflorescence (Fig. 52-57s).

perennial — plant that lives more than two years.

perianth — collectively all the sepals and petals, or tepals, of flower.

petal — a member of the second set of floral leaves (corolla). (Fig. 39-48f).

petaloid — petal-like.

petiolate — having a leaf stalk.

petiole — stalk of leaf. (Fig. 1-11c).

pinnate — two rows of lateral branches, or parts along axis. (Fig. 2 & 10).

pinnatifid — leaves more or less deeply cut to mid-rib. (Fig. 12).

pinnatilobate — with pinnately arranged lobes. (Fig. 10).

pistil — female organ of flower, composed of one or more carpels. (Fig. 39a, b, c, & 51a, c).

plaited — folded.

pod — the fruit of legumes, a dry fruit opening along two lines in a single carpel. (Fig. 62).

pome — fruit with core (like apple). (Fig. 59).

pubescent — bearing hairs of any sort.

pungent — (touch) sharp pointed; (odor or taste) sharp, acrid, penetrating.

raceme — inflorescence in which pedicels are distributed along axis, lower flowers opening first. (Fig. 52).

ray — the small flower (floret) of the heads of the family *Compositae* (Fig. 47) which has a flat corolla. (Fig. 48f).

reflexed — sharply bent back.

reniform — kidney shaped. (Fig. 26).

repand — slightly and irregularly wavy.

rhombic — somewhat diamond shaped.

rosette — cluster of leaves arranged in circle, in a basal position.

sagittate — arrowhead shaped. (Fig. 35).

salverform — flower with long, narrow tube, limb spreading at right angles (Fig. 43).

samara—a winged one seeded dry fruit. (Fig. 61).

scape—flowering stem of plant without leaves.

scarious—thin, dry and chaffy in texture, not green.

scorpoid—coiled in flat spiral, uncoiling with development.

scurfy—covered with minute scales or granules.

sepals—members of outermost floral leaves (calyx), usually green. (Fig. 39, 40, 44-46g).

serrate—saw-like, margin evenly and sharply indented. (Fig. 14).

serrulate—finely saw-toothed.

sessile—without a stalk.

silicle—characteristic capsule of *Cruciferae* family member when length is not more than twice width.

silique—characteristic capsule of *Cruciferae* family member when length is several times greater than width. (Fig. 64).

simple—(leaves, stems) having but one blade or main axis; (flowers) rachis unbranched. (Fig. 1, 7-35).

sinuate—with a wavy margin.

spathe—bract or leafy part (Fig. 49l) sheathing a flower or flower cluster (spadix) (Fig. 49m).

spatulate—shaped like a flattened spoon. (Fig. 21).

spikelet—the inflorescence of grasses. (Fig. 50 & 51).

spinose—having character of spine.

stamen—male organ of flower, bearing pollen. (Fig. 39d, e).

staminiodium—imperfect or sterile stamen, not bearing pollen.

stipule—one of a pair of basal appendages on many leaves. (Fig. 1b).

styles—narrow extension of pistil above ovary, bearing stigma. (Fig. 39b).

succulent—pulpy, juicy.

sympetalous—with petals connate, at least toward base. (Fig. 41-46, 48f).

tendril—a slender, coiling or twining organ, by which plant supports itself. (Fig. 6).

tepal—petal or sepal, or members of undifferentiated perianth.

terete—round in cross-section.

ternate—divided into threes. (Fig. 4).

tomentose—with minute wooly hairs.

truncate—apex or base as though cut squarely across. (Fig. 32).

tuber—short and fleshy underground stem. (Fig. 36).

turbinate—top-shaped.

umbel—inflorescence in which pedicels all spring from same point. (Fig. 57).

umbellate—in umbels.

vernation—arrangement of leaves in bud.

verticillate—arranged in verticils or whorls. (Fig. 9).

whorl—ring of three or more similar structures radiating from node or common point. (Fig. 9).

zygomorphic—bilaterally symmetrical. (Fig. 44, 45, 48).

Illustrations of Flower Parts and Terms

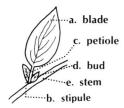

a. blade
c. petiole
d. bud
e. stem
b. stipule

1. Simple Leaf

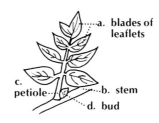

a. blades of leaflets
c. petiole
b. stem
d. bud

2. Pinnately Compound Leaf

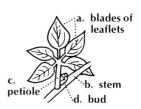

a. blades of leaflets
c. petiole
b. stem
d. bud

3. Palmately Compound Leaf

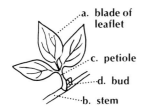

a. blade of leaflet
c. petiole
d. bud
b. stem

4. Ternate Compound Leaf

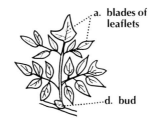

a. blades of leaflets
d. bud

5. Bipinnate Leaf

6. Tendril

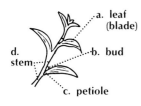

a. leaf (blade)
d. stem
b. bud
c. petiole

7. Alternate Leaves

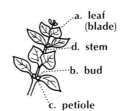

a. leaf (blade)
d. stem
b. bud
c. petiole

8. Opposite Leaves

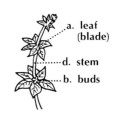

a. leaf (blade)
d. stem
b. buds

9. Whorled Leaves

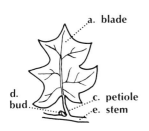

a. blade
d. bud
c. petiole
e. stem

10. Pinnately Lobed Leaf

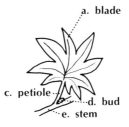

a. blade
c. petiole
d. bud
e. stem

11. Palmately Lobed Leaf

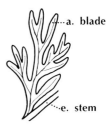

a. blade
e. stem

12. Dissected Pinnatifid

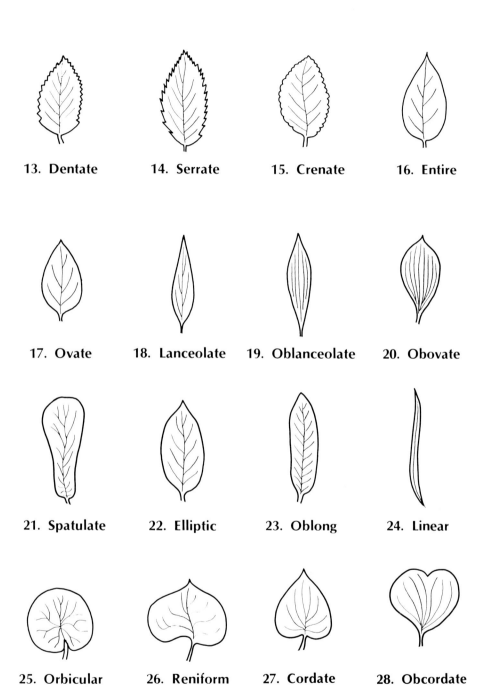

13. Dentate   14. Serrate   15. Crenate   16. Entire

17. Ovate   18. Lanceolate   19. Oblanceolate   20. Obovate

21. Spatulate   22. Elliptic   23. Oblong   24. Linear

25. Orbicular   26. Reniform   27. Cordate   28. Obcordate

29. Acuminate

30. Acute

31. Obtuse

32. Truncate

33. Cuneate

34. Auriculate

35. Sagittate

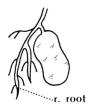

r. root

36. Tuber

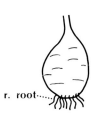

r. root

37. Corm

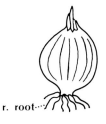

r. root

38. Bulb

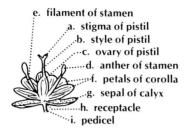

e. filament of stamen
a. stigma of pistil
b. style of pistil
c. ovary of pistil
d. anther of stamen
f. petals of corolla
g. sepal of calyx
h. receptacle
i. pedicel

39. Flower with Superior Ovary

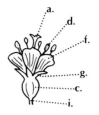

40. Flower with Inferior Ovary

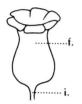

41. Campanulate

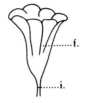

42. Funnelform

43. Salverform

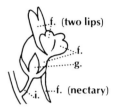

44. Bilabiate

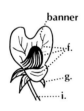

banner

45. Papilionaceous

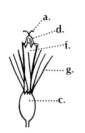

46. Disk Floret of Composite

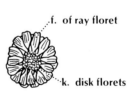

f. of ray floret

k. disk florets

47. Composite

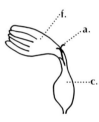

48. Ray Floret of Composite

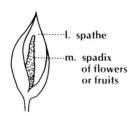

l. spathe
m. spadix of flowers or fruits

49. Spathe & Spadix

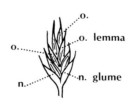

o. lemma

n. glume

50. Spikelet of Grass

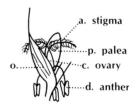

a. stigma
p. palea
c. ovary
d. anther

51. Floret of Grass Spikelet

16

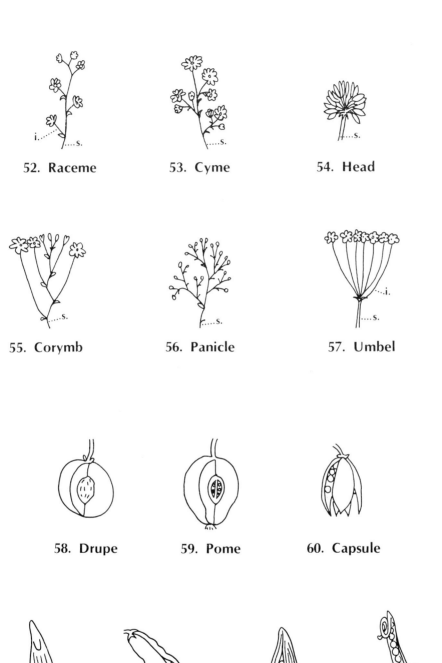

52. **Raceme**

53. **Cyme**

54. **Head**

55. **Corymb**

56. **Panicle**

57. **Umbel**

58. **Drupe**

59. **Pome**

60. **Capsule**

61. **Samara**

62. **Pod**

63. **Follicle**

64. **Silique**

Section I

Woody Plants:
Trees, Shrubs, and Vines

Western Juniper
Cypress Family (*Cupressaceae*)   *Juniperus occidentalis*

Name source: *Juniperus* — Latin name for Juniper.

Description: Small tree, shape variable. Bark brown and shredding. Leaves in threes, 1.5-3 mm long. Early leaves much longer, linear and sharp tipped. Closely appressed, resinous glandular (sticky) on back. Staminate (pollen bearing) cones, 2-4 mm long. Female cones berry-like, globuse or oval, blue when mature, 6-8 mm long, 2-5 seeded. Wood durable, used mostly for fence posts. Berries edible raw or dried, contain oil used for flavoring.

Habitat: Desert foothills and lower mountains. Spreading rapidly because of lack of fire. Range: Central Washington and Oregon to Nevada, southwestern Idaho, and southern California.

Curl-leaf Mountain Mahogany
Rose Family (*Rosaceae*)   *Cercocarpus ledifolius*

Name source: *Kerkos* — tail, *carpos* — fruit, referring to persistent long styles on fruit.

Description: Leaves entire, narrowly elliptic to elliptic-lanceolate, 2-3 cm long, glabrous and shining above and yellow tomentose below, with acute tips and bases, margins generally revolute. Flowers perfect, no petals, several in axillary clusters on short lateral shoots. Calyx turbinate, 3-8 mm. Hypanthium persistent around, but free of ovary, bearing near summit 20-30 stamens, 5 lobes. 1 pistil, 1 carpellary, style exserted, elongate and plumose in fruit. Large shrub to small tree. Preferred and nutritious browse for Big-horn sheep and Mule deer.

Range: Southeastern Washington to Montana, Colorado. Arizona and California. Habitat: Open rocky ridges. Season: April — May.

20

Bushy Eriogonum, Slenderbush Buckwheat
Buckwheat Family (*Polygonaceae*)   *Eriogonum microthecium*

Name source: *Erion* — wool; *gonu* — knee, referring to hairy stems and their nodes.

Description: Erect or decumbent branched shrub, young branches tomentose. Leaves oblanceolate to linear-oblong, acute or sharp, margins often involute, glabrate above, white tomentous beneath, 1.5-3 cm long, on short petioles. Inflorescence dense, 3-6 times branched, the ultimate branches very short, each bearing a single involucre, narrowly turbinate 2-3 mm long, few flowered. Flowers white to yellow to pink, 2-3 mm long. Perianth 6-parted at base, stamens 9, 3 carpels.

Habitat: Dry open ground. Range: North central Washington to Montana to New Mexico and California on east side of Cascades. Season: June — October.

Shadscale, Spiny Saltbush, Sheepfat
Goosefoot Family (*Chenopodiaceae*)   *Atriplex confertifolia*

Name source: *Atriplex* — Latin name for plant; *confertifolia* — closely set leaves.

Description: Plants dioecious, 2-12 dm tall. Branches many, rigid, spiny. Leaves grayish-whitish scurfy, broadly ovate to oval, entire, short-petioled to subsessile.

Very valuable browse in desert areas. Zuni Indians in New Mexico ground roots and blossoms and mixed with saliva for ant bites (A. canescens). Seeds and young shoots are edible.

Habitat: Dry alkaline soils. Range: Wasco County, Oregon south to California, east to southern and central Idaho to southern Montana to the Dakotas, Wyoming, Colorado, and New Mexico. Season: April-July.

Russian Thistle, Tumbleweed, Wind Witch
Goosefoot Family (*Chenopodiaceae*)   *Salsola kali*

Name source: *Salsus* — salt, referring to habitat and taste.

Description: Bushy branched annual, stem stout, 2-6 dm high. Leaves narrowly linear 2-7 cm long, leaves of smaller branches much shorter, awl shaped, sharp tipped. Plant green to pink to lavender depending in part on season. Stem breaks off, plant rolls in the wind becoming yellowish light gray in color. Bracts become spinescent. Flowers solitary in upper axils, perfect, perianth membranaceous.

Habitat: Dry soil or climate, often alkaline open areas, favored by disturbance, commonly on road shoulders. Range: Mostly east of Cascades in United States and southern Canada. Season: Late August-late September.

Oregon Grape, Grape Root, Mountain Grape
Barberry Family (*Berberidaceae*)   *Berberis aquifolium*

Name source: *Berberis* — from Arabic, *berberys,* name for plant; *aquifolium* — pointed leaves.

Description: Shrub, clustered, 1.5-30 dm high. Leaflets deep green above, pale beneath, 5-9 per leaf, oblong to ovate or ovate-lanceolate, 3-10 cm long, 2-5 cm broad, with 12-20 spinose teeth. Flower bright yellow. Sepals oblong, 7-8 mm long. Berries deep blue. The berries may be eaten raw, in jellies, or they can be made into a beverage. The roots can be made into a dye (yellow), or a tonic or alterative.

Habitat: Coniferous woods to sagebrush slopes. Range: Southern British Columbia and northern Washington to northeastern Idaho. South from east base of Cascades to southern Willamette Valley, Oregon. Season: March-May.

Squaw Currant, White Squaw Currant, Sheep Currant
Currant, Gooseberry Family (*Grossulariaceae*)   *Ribes cereum*

Name source: *Ribes* — Arabic name of plant *ribas; cereum* — resembling wax.

Description: Spreading or rounded erect, intricately branched, 5-15 dm. Leaves almost reniform to broadly cuneate, flabellate, cordate at base, 1-3 cm broad, shallowly lobed or toothed (3-5). Petiole as long as blade, or shorter. Flowers sticky. Calyx white or pinkish, hypanthium cylindric, 8-10 mm long, lobes spreading, recurved, 1.5-3 mm. Petals 1-2 mm. Berry bright red, 6-8 mm. Ribes species may be eaten fresh, canned, in pies, jams, jellies, and juice. Ribes cereum was used by Indians. Too many cause sickness; considered to be poor as fruit.

Habitat: From sagebrush desert to subalpine ridges. Range: East slopes of Cascades from British Columbia through Oregon to southern California. East to Montana, Nebraska, Colorado, New Mexico, Arizona, and South Dakota. Season: April-July.

Umatilla Gooseberry
Gooseberry, Currant Family (*Grossulariaceae*)   *Ribes cognatum*

Name source: From *ribas* — Arabic name for plant.

Description: Much branched, 2-4 m tall. Spines 10-15 mm, straight. Leaf blades broadly ovate, 1.5-4 cm broad, deeply lobed (3-5), lobes oblong, rounded with 5-9 dentations. Petioles mostly shorter than blades. Hypanthium greenish-white to pinkish, cylindric, 4-6 mm, about ⅔ length of to as long as hypanthium, oblong, obtuse to rounded. Stamens equaling to slightly longer than petals, 3-3.5 mm. Berry red, drying to black, palatable.

Habitat: Stream banks. Range: Umatilla River and tributaries to Wheeler County, Wallowa Mountains and eastern Washington, north central Idaho. Season: Late March-early June.

Western Black Currant
Gooseberry, Currant Family (*Grossulariaceae*)   *Ribes hudsonianum*

Name source: *Ribas* — Arabic name for plants.

Description: Erect, 0.5-2 m high, covered with yellow crystalline shining glands, having a strong sweet unpleasant odor. Leaves broadly cordate, 3.5-12 cm broad with 3-5 deltoid lobes, these lobes bicrenate to dentate. Calyx saucer-shaped, 7-9 mm wide, white. Sepals 1-1.5 mm long, triangular, 3-4 mm wide. Petals white, 1.5 mm. Berry black, very bitter, not at all good.

Habitat: Stream bank, moist woods, and margins of meadows in mountains. Range: Alaska to northern California, eastern Cascades. East to Ontario, Minnesota, and Utah. Season: June-August.

Juneberry, Serviceberry, Shadberry
Rose Family (*Rosaceae*)   *Amelanchier alnifolia*

Name source: *Alnifolia* — with leaves like alder.

Description: Shrub or tree, usually 1-5 m (sometimes to 10 m) tall. Leaves slender, petioled, 10-20 mm; blades oval, oblong, elliptic-oblong, 2-4 cm long, 1/2 to 5/6 as broad, cuneate to rounded, to subcordate, serrate along nearly whole margin or only at tip. Hypanthium 1-2 mm. Petals white (occasionally pinkish), linear to linear-oblanceolate, 10-20 mm long, 2-6 mm broad. Stamens 12-15, or commonly 20. Styles usually 5. Fruit 10-14 mm long, generally dark purplish, rather juicy, palatable. Extremely variable, length of calyx lobes, petals, styles, anthers, number of styles, shape and texture of leaves all vary.

Berries may be eaten raw, in pies, pudding, and jelly. Indians dried berries for winter use — crushed into cake from which pieces are broken off. Used in pemmican. Eye wash made from boiled inner bark. Can be dried and eaten like raisins; or cooked into puree or jam.

Habitat: Open woods, canyons, hillsides, from sea level to subalpine. Range: Southern Alaska south to California, east to Alberta, Dakotas, Nebraska, Colorado, New Mexico, Arizona. Season: April-July.

Utah Serviceberry
Rose Family (*Rosaceae*)   *Amelanchier utahensis*

Name source: *Utahensis* — from Utah.

Description: Very similar to A. alnifolia, but usually shorter and irregularly branched, 0.5-4 m. Leaf blades yellowish-green and rather coriaceous (paler beneath), oval or oblong-elliptic to broadly obovate, 1.5 to 3 cm long, serrate. Petals white to pink in bud, cuneate-oblanceolate, elliptic, 6-9 mm long, to 4 mm broad. Stamens usually about 15. Styles 4. Fruit to 10 mm, dark purple and fleshy, or dry and more reddish.

Habitat: Rimrock, valleys, gullies, and hillsides from sagebrush desert to middle elevation in mountains. Range: Central Idaho south to Baja and Sonora; west to southeastern Oregon, Nevada, and southeastern California; east to Montana, Wyoming, Colorado, New Mexico, and west Texas. Occasionally in central Oregon (Wheeler County) and Yakima, Washington. Season: May-July.

Bitter Cherry
Rose Family (*Rosaceae*)

Prunus emarginata

Name source: *Prunus* — ancient Latin name for plum; *emarginata* — having a notch cut out.

Description: Shrub 1-5 m to tree 15 m tall. Young twigs reddish. Leaves petioled, 5-12 mm, blades elliptic or oblong to oblong-obovate, obovate, or oblanceolate, crenulate to serrate, 2-8 cm long. Petals obovate to obovate-lanceolate, 4-7 mm long. Sepals oblong, obtuse, 2 mm. Stamens about 20. Fruit 5-8 mm diameter, bright red to black, very bitter and astringent.

Leaves, bark, seeds contain substance that breaks down into cyanide (Cyanogenic glycoside amygdalin). Children have been poisoned by eating seeds, chewing twigs, drinking "tea" from leaves. Symptoms: difficult breathing, paralysis of voice, twitching, spasms, coma of short duration and death, which can occur suddenly without warning. Genus contains plums and cherries.

Habitat: Mountain woods and along watercourses, grassland, and sagebrush desert. Range: British Columbia south to southern California, east to Montana, Wyoming, Utah, and Arizona. Season: April — June.

Bitter Brush, Antelope Brush
Rose Family (*Rosaceae*)   *Purshia tridentata*

Name source: *Purshia* — for F.T. Pursh (1774-1820), author of early American Flora; *tridentata* — 3 toothed.

Description: Rigidly branched shrub, 1-3 m. Leaves cuneate, 5-30 mm, 3-lobed, thick, white beneath, dark green above. Sepals 3-4 mm. Petals 5, pale yellow, spatulate-obovate, 6-9 mm long. Stamens about 25. Pistil 1.

One of the best browse plants in western United States. Used ornamentally for floral arrangements. The leaves were used by Indians as cough medicine. This plant can respond to local differences; for example, the branches near rocks or the ground may bloom while the others are still in bud, due to the difference in heat absorption. It often regenerates roots and branches where old branches touch the ground. It generally will not sprout after a fire.

Habitat: Dry, rocky ground, grassland, and sagebrush-juniper woods to Ponderosa pine forest. Range: British Columbia south along east side of Cascades to central California, east to western Montana, Wyoming, Colorado, and New Mexico. Season: May-June.

31

Spalding's Rose, Wild Rose
Rose Family (*Rosaceae*)   *Rosa nutkana*

Name source: *Rosa* — classic Latin name; *nutkana* — Nootka Sound, British Columbia.

Description: Difficult Genus, hybridizes easily and readily. Shrub 1-2 m tall, not always too prickly. Leaflets mostly 5-7, elliptic or ovate, serrate or double serrate, 1-7 cm long and 0.7-4.5 cm broad. Flowers large. Sepals mostly 5, mostly 1.5-4 cm long, 3-6 mm wide at base. Petals mostly 5 except in cultivated species where double and flowers poly-petaled, light pink to deep rose, 2.5-4 cm long. Hips orange to purplish. Very attractive in flower and fruit. R. nutkana (especially Spaldingii) considered best. The fruit, known as hips, can be eaten raw, stewed, candied, or made into preserves or tea. The hips and petals are often made into wine. The leaves and petals also have some astringent properties.

Habitat: Stream bank, mostly wooded region. Range: Alaska and British Columbia south to northern California. In eastern Oregon to Blue Mountains, and Rocky Mountains to Colorado and Utah. Season: May — July.

Gray Ball Sage
Mint Family (*Labiatae*)   *Salvia dorrii*

Name source: *Salvia* — ancient Latin name for sage.

Description: Low, much branched shrubs, aromatic, 2-8 dm tall, often broader than high, branches rigid. Leaves numerous, silvery, mealy, oblanceolate or elliptic to spatulate or obovate, entire, 1.5-3 cm long. Flowers dense, bright blue or violet to (rarely) white, 1-1.5 cm long, lower lip spreading (3-lobed), larger than upper 2 lobes. Stamens 2, long, exserted. The oil of the leaves and seeds is used as flavoring and convulsant. The seeds can be eaten raw or parched. The parched seeds can be ground into a flour. A spoonful of the seeds stirred into a glass of water is said to make a good drink.

Habitat: Dry hillsides, often with sagebrush. Range: Washington and Oregon east of Cascades to California, southwestern Idaho, and Arizona. Season: May-July.

Big Sagebrush
Composite Family (*Compositae*)   *Artemesia tridentata*

Name source: *Artemesia* — ancient common name of some of the species of this genus.

Description: Aromatic gray-leaved shrub. Alternate gray-tomentose leaves, cuneate, 3-toothed and widest at tip, persistent. Panicle-shaped inflorescence. Heads small, numerous, discoid, 3-6 flowered. Involucral bracts dry, imbricate, canescent. Bark gray and shredded. Seeds or fruits can be dried and pounded into meal. Tea of leaves or stems used for colds in nose and throat.

Habitat: Dry plains and hills to timberline. Increases with grazing intensity and with fire protection. Range: Interior British Columbia to Baja California, east to North Dakota and New Mexico. Season: July-October.

Gray Rabbitbrush
Composite Family (*Compositae*)   *Chrysothamnus nauseosus*

Name source: *Chryso*—yellow, gold.

Description: Shrub. Twigs covered with felt-like tomentum, gray-green to white. Alternate, sessile, narrow to linear entire leaves, whitish. Many small discoid narrow heads with about 5 perfect, yellow flowers. Involucral bracts, acute, imbricate, arranged in about 5 vertical ranks. Receptacle naked. Pappus of capillary bristles.

Habitat: Dry open ground, favored by disturbance, often common along road shoulders. Range: British Columbia and Alberta through central Washington and Oregon to California and northern California. East to northern Great Plains. Season: Early August-early September.

Small Bindweed, Field Bindweed, Field Morning-glory, Orchard Morning-glory
Morning-glory Family (*Convolvulaceae*)   *Convolvulus arvensis*

Name source: Latin. *Convolvulus — convolvere,* meaning to twine.

Description: Perennial with trailing or twining stems, 2-20 dm long. Leaves simple, alternate. Leaf blades ovate-lanceolate to truncate or more commonly sagittate, the basal ones 2-6 cm long. Petiole 5-30 mm. Flower funnelform, large and showy. Corolla plaited, white to pinkish or purplish, 1.5-2.5 cm long. Calyx lobed, 4-5 mm, oblong, ovate. Root contains cathartic properties.

Habitat: Dry roadside. Range: Very well established in much of North America. Introduced from Europe. Season: May-October.

Section II

Herbs

1. Flower parts in threes or sixes, colors various
2. Flowers bilaterally symmetrical, colors various
3. Flowers in heads: Compositae family, colors various
4. Flowers green, white, cream, yellow, orange or red
5. Flowers pink, lavender, violet, purple, or blue

Hooker's Onion
Lily Family (*Liliaceae*)   *Allium acuminatum*

Name source: *Allium*—Latin name for garlic; *acuminatum*—long pointed.

Description: Stem 1-3 dm tall, round. Leaves 2 or more, 1-3 mm broad, shorter than stem, often withering at or before flowering. Umbel open, 7-30-flowered. Flowers deep rose-purple or pink to white, 8-17 mm long, lanceolate, acuminate.

The bulb is edible, and according to people who eat such things, it tastes rather like garlic. A little of the bulb or leaf can be used as seasoning. The juice boiled down has been used as a cure for colds and sore throats. Bulbs have been placed in the ear to cure earaches and against teeth to cure toothaches. The juice of the bulbs has been used in dressing wounds. The bulbs can be dried and stored. Plants can be rubbed on the skin as an insect repellent. Eating the bulbs or leaves by cattle causes bad flavoring in milk.

Habitat: Dry, open, rocky ground, hills and plains. Range: East of Cascades in Washington and Oregon to southern Wyoming, western Colorado, Arizona, and northern California. Season: May—July.

Tolmie's Onion
Lily Family (*Liliaceae*)

Allium tolmiei

Name source: *Allium* — Latin name for garlic.

Description: Scape 2-25 cm tall. Leaves 2, flat, thick, commonly falcate, 4-10 mm wide, usually entire, up to 2 times length of stem, green at flowering. Umbel 25-60-flowered. Flowers light rose-purple to white with dark stripes, segments lanceolate-acute, 6-12 mm long.

Habitat: Rocky, gravelly, clay soils, generally with sparse cover. Range: Eastern Oregon, southeastern Washington and western Idaho to northeastern California. Season: April — June.

39

Large Flowered Brodiaea
Lily Family (*Liliaceae*)   *Brodiaea douglasii*

Name source: *Brodiaea* — for James J. Brodie, Scotch Botanist.

Description: Scape 2-7 dm tall. Leaves 1-2, 3-10 mm broad, 2.5-5 dm long, green at flowering. Flowers 8-16 in an open umbel, deep to light blue with a deeper midvein, tubular campanulate, lobes ½ + inflated tube, tube 9-12 mm long. Perianth segments in 2 series. 6 fertile stamens in 2 series. Often confused with Wild Onion, Camas.

Eaten by Indians and explorers. Nez Perce Indians gathered plants in quantities and ate them raw or cooked. Boiled, they are sweet, nutlike. Seed pods are green. Animals feed on greens and corms.

Habitat: Grasslands and sagebrush desert to Ponderosa pine forests. Dry to moist soils. Range: Southern British Columbia to southern Oregon (on east side of Cascades). East to Idaho, Montana, and western Wyoming and northern Utah. Season: April — July.

Brodiaea Lily, Howell's Brodiaea
Lily Family (*Liliaceae*)   *Brodiaea howellii*

Name source: *Brodiaea*—for James J. Brodie; Scotch Botanist; *howellii*—for Joseph Howell.

Description: Perianth white with midvein, the tube slenderly campanulate, 7-10 mm long, 2 series of segments equal in length. Filaments very unequal, but set at same level, broad and thick. The corm of this plant is edible raw or cooked. It is said to taste best when cooked slowly to bring out the sweetness. The tender seed pods make a good green.

Habitat: Dry, rocky ground; coastal bluffs and prairies to sagebrush desert and lower hills. Range: Southwestern British Columbia to southwestern Oregon to east base of Cascades— Gilliam County, Oregon. Season: April—June.

Sagebrush Mariposa, Green-banded Star Tulip, Green-banded Mariposa Lily
Lily Family (*Liliaceae*) *Calochortus macrocarpus*

Name source: *Kalo*—beautiful; *chortos*—grass.

Description: Perennial from bulb. Stem 3-7 dm tall, stout, stiffly erect. Leaves 3-5, withering by time of flowering. Flowers 1-3. Three petals, narrowly obovate, abruptly accuminate 3-6 cm long. Bright lilac to white with yellow base, with green stripe down the middle. Bulbs are edible raw or cooked. Also ground into flour. Use only in emergencies.

Habitat: Arid areas. Range: East side of Cascades to southcentral British Columbia, to southwestern Montana, Nevada, northern Mexico and northeastern California. Season: Late June—mid-July.

Common Camas, Quamash, Camas Root, Quamass Root, Squamash
Lily Family (*Liliaceae*)   *Camassia quamash*

Name source: *Camassia, quamash* — Indian names for camas and quamash. Name given to Camas, Idaho; Camas Prairie, Idaho; Camas Hot Springs, Montana.

Description: Scape often stout, 2-7 dm tall. Leaves 8-20 mm broad, shorter than scape. Raceme few- to many-flowered. Perianth dark purplish blue to light blue. Segments 10-35 mm long. Confused with Zygadenus and Brodiaea.

Bulbs can be eaten raw, baked (cooked in rock ovens), roasted, boiled (potato-like, gummy), or dried. Camas bulbs were the chief vegetable in the diet of the Indians and early settlers. It is said that the reason that the Nez Perce under Chief Joseph left their reservation was to go south to collect Camas bulbs.

Habitat: Wet meadow; moist areas where dry by late spring. Range: British Columbia south on both sides of the Cascades to California. East to southwestern Alberta, Montana, Wyoming, Utah. Season: April — June.

Yellow Fawn's Lily, Yellow Adderstongue, Dogtooth Violet
Lily Family (*Liliaceae*)   *Erythronium grandiflorum*

Name source: Greek. *Erythro*—red, referring to red flowers of some species; *grandiflorum*—large flower.

Description: Leaves basal, petiolate to subsessile, narrowly to broadly elliptic, 7-20 cm long with broad petioles. Tepals lanceolate, 2.5-5 cm long, pale yellow to cream to golden. Stamens 6 in 2 slightly unlike sets.

The Indians ate the bulbs boiled or dried for the winter. The leaves can be eaten as greens. The fresh green seed pods taste like string beans when boiled.

Habitat: Moist stream-bank; sagebrush slopes to mountain forests, sometimes near timber-line. Range: Southern British Columbia, Olympic and Cascade Mountains of Washington and northern Oregon. East to Montana, Wyoming, Colorado. In Oregon—east of Cascades. Season: March—August (depends on elevation).

Yellow Bell, Yellow Fritillary
Lily Family (*Liliaceae*)   *Fritillaria pudica*

Name source: Latin. *Fritillus*—dice box, referring to capsule; *pudica*—bashful or modest, so named because the blossoms turn reddish with age.

Description: Perennial herb. Stems mostly 8-30 cm tall. Leaves 2-8, usually subopposite or alternate. Flowers usually solitary, sometimes (rarely) 2-3, narrowly campanulate, yellow, often purple or brownish streaked near base, fading to red or purple with age. Tepals oblong-lanceolate to oblanceolate, 10-26 mm long, 4-10 mm broad. Stamens 6. Sometimes confused with Erythronium.

The bulbs of this plant can be eaten either cooked or raw. Cooked they are said to taste like rice; raw they are said to taste like potatoes. They can also be dried for storage. The green pods can be eaten cooked or raw.

Habitat: Dry Hilltop; grasslands and sagebrush desert to Ponderosa pine or mixed conifer forests. Range: British Columbia south to east of Cascades to northern California. East to Alberta, Idaho, Montana, Wyoming, Utah, Nevada. Season: March—June.

Poison Camas, Death Camas, Ward Lily, White Camas, Poison Sego, Deadly Zygadene
Lily Family (*Liliaceae*)   *Zigadenus venenosus*

Name source: Greek. *Zugon*—yoke, *aden*—gland, refers to paired glands in some (most) species; *venenosus*—very poisonous.

Description: Perennial herbs 2-6 dm tall. Leaves mostly basal, 1-3 dm long. Perianth white to cream-colored campanulate. Tepals 7, the outer 4.5-5 mm (5-7), ovate, the inner about 0.5 mm longer. Stamens 6.

Very poisonous to man and livestock. Sheep are more affected because they are more apt to eat it; hogs are said to be immune. Indians and early settlers were poisoned when they mistook the plants or bulbs for true Camas. The plants are quite different in flower, but are easy to mistake when just looking at the bulbs. Symptoms of poisoning: muscular weakness, slow heartbeat, subnormal temperature, upset stomach, vomiting, diarrhea, excessive watering of the mouth.

Habitat: Dry meadow—coastal prairies and rocky bluffs to grassy hillsides, sagebrush, and montane forest in exposed places. Range: Southern British Columbia to Baja. East to Alberta, southwestern Saskatchewan, Dakotas, Nebraska, Colorado. Season: March—July.

46

Grass Widows, Purple-eyed Grass
Iris Family (*Iridaceae*)

Sisyrinchium douglasii

Name source: *Sisyrinchium*—name used by Theophrastus for some Iris-like plant.

Description: Stems single or from small clusters, 15-30 cm high. Leaves 2-3, blades grasslike, shorter than stem, 1.5-3 mm wide. Bract of spathe leaf-like, overlapping flowers. Flowers mostly 2, but occasionally 1 or 3. Perianth of 6 similar segments, deep reddish purple to white, 15-22 mm long. Confused with Dodecatheon.

Habitat: Open field; prairies, meadows, grass, hillsides to rocky slopes in sagebrush to oak or Ponderosa pine woodland—apparently dry places, but moist in early spring. From near sea level to above 6,000 feet. Range: Vancouver Island south on both sides of Cascades to California. East to Nevada. Season: March—June.

47

Western Iris, Blue Flag, Water Flag, Fleur-de-lis, Snake Lily
Iris Family (*Iridaceae*)

Iris missouriensis

Name source: Greek. *Iris* — popularly believed for rainbow, based on bright colors of flowers; *missouriensis* — from the Missouri River. Iris (fleur-de-lis) is the emblem of France.

Description: Stems nearly round, simple, 2-6 dm tall. Leaves often only 1, 2-4 dm, basal. Flowers usually 2, pale to deep blue, variegated. Perianth tube flared above, 5-12 mm long. Sepals spreading, reflexed, oblanceolate, 5-6 cm long. Petals slightly less than sepals.

A clump of Iris is generally a good sign of water close to the surface of the ground. The root-stocks may cause skin irritation and, if eaten, cause a severe burning of the mouth and throat that lasts for hours (the first taste is said to be good, but is soon burning). The roots were ground by Indians, mixed with animal bile, and warmed for several days by a fire in a gall bladder. Arrow points were then dipped into the mixture. It is reported by old Indians that many warriors only slightly wounded by such arrows died within 3 to 7 days.

Habitat: Damp meadows, streambanks. The common species east of Cascades in seepage areas in sagebrush desert and pine forest. Range: British Columbia to California. East of Cascades. East to Dakotas, south to New Mexico. Season: May — early June.

Upland Larkspur
Buttercup Family (*Ranunculaceae*)   *Delphinium nuttalianum*

Name source: Latinized form of Greek, *Delphinion,* for Larkspur, used by Dioscorides.

Description: Stems usually single, 1.5-4.5 dm high. Leaves few, orbicular, mostly basal, long-petioled, 2-6 cm broad, 3-5 parted into linear or oblong-lanceolate lobes. Sepals from white or pale grayish-blue to deep bluish-purple. Spur from not quite as long to twice as long as sepal. Lower petals white to blue.

Larkspur is very poisonous to cattle, especially during the spring. It is second only to loco-weed in cattle losses. It is apparently not poisonous to sheep; they have even been used to eat it out of cattle ranges. Delphinium species may have delphinine, delphineidine, ajacine, and other alkaloids. Symptoms: stomach upsets, nervous symptoms, depression. Fatal in large quantities. Tincture of delphinium is used externally to kill parasites.

Habitat: Talus slope. Sagebrush desert to mountain valleys and slopes, usually rock soil, well drained. Range: Southwest British Columbia to northern California; east to Alberta. Montana, Wyoming, Nebraska, and south to Colorado and Arizona. Season: March—July.

49

Milk Vetch, Crow Toe, Locoweed, Rattle Pod
Pea Family (*Leguminosae*)   *Astragalus spp.*

Name source: Ancient Greek name for some leguminous plant, possibly from *astragalos,* name for bone in ankle, in reference to pod or leaf shape.

Description: Annual or perennial herbs. Leaves odd-pinnate, with several to many leaflets. Calyx 5-toothed. Keel obtuse, pod often inflated, banner well reflexed, wings mostly greater than keel, generally less than banner but sometimes equaling or exceeding it. Flowers white, purple, yellow, showy. Large genus—2,000+ species; 550 in North America. Many species very localized. This genus has a large number of leaflets and all the stamen filaments but one grow together and form a papery sheath around the ovary. Several species are known to be poisonous to livestock. Some are always poisonous, others only on selenium soils. Toxic even when dry. Locoweed is habitforming for cattle.

Habitat: Dry open ground. Range: Highly developed in steppe, desert, and cold montane climates of northern United States.

Wild Pea, Sweet Pea
Pea Family (*Leguminosae*)   *Lathyrus spp.*

Name source: Ancient Greek name for some member of Leguminosae family.

Description: Perennial or occasionally annual. Usually vines. Leaves pinnately compound, 2-8 leaflets. Calyx teeth nearly equal; banner generally at 90 degrees to wings and keel; keel not beaked.

This genus is different from *Astragalus* (Milk Vetches) in that it has a tendril on the tip of its leaf, whereas the milk vetches have another leaflet. It is most similar to the genus *Vicia* (true vetches), but the members of *Lathyrus* tend to have a small non-functional tendril, as opposed to a large active one, and a larger, broader flower. The seeds are poisonous, causing paralysis, slow and weak pulse, shallow breathing, and convulsions.

Habitat: Damp shaded hillside. Range: Nearly all of the North Temperate Zone.

Small-flowered Lupine
Pea Family (*Leguminosae*)   *Lupinus micranthus*

Name source: *Lupinus*— from Latin *lupus,* meaning wolf; *micranthus*— small, minute flowers.

Description: Simple to freely branched, 1-4 dm tall. Leaves palmately compound, 5-8 leaflets, linear to oblanceolate, 1.5-3 cm long, 2/5-4/5 length of petiole, glabrous above, hairy below. Calyx strongly bilabiate, lips about 3 mm long. Flower 8-10 mm long, bluish, banner often white centered, banner margins scarcely reflexed. Keel ciliate on upper half. Stamens 10. Pods flattened, hairy. Probably most chaotic genus in area. Species very plastic, varying bewilderingly; free interbreeding. Very showy. Correct names doubtful (Hitchcock).

Habitat: Sandy open ground. Range: West of Cascades from British Columbia to southern California; up Columbia Gorge to northeastern Oregon. Season: March—June.

Spurred Lupine
Pea Family (*Leguminosae*)   *Lupinus laxiflorus*

Name source: *Lupinus* —from Latin *lupus,* meaning wolf; *laxiflorus* —loose, limp flowers.

Description: Perennial; numerous erect spreading branches, 2-8 dm tall. Leaves mostly cauline, lower petiole 2-4 times blades, upper often ½ as long. Leaflets 7-11, linear to oblong-oblanceolate, abruptly pointed, 3-7 cm long, hairy on both sides. Calyx with conspicuous spur 1-3 mm long. Corolla 10-12 mm long, white to cream all over or with tinge of bluish, pinkish, or violet to rose or purple, often varying on same plant. Banner very hairy on upper side above middle; keel ciliate most of length; pods more or less silky. Variable in flower color, hair on banner, and development of spur.

Habitat: Sagebrush and Ponderosa pine country. Range: East of Cascades from Washington to California, east to Idaho, Montana, Utah, and Nevada. Season: May-July.

Dry-ground Lupine
Pea Family (*Leguminosae*) *Lupinus lepidus*

Name source: *Lupinus* — from Latin *lupus*, meaning wolf.

Description: Low and spreading to erect, 1-2 dm, erect stems seldom as long as petioles of lower-most leaves. Leaves largely basal, petioles 2-5 times length of blades. Leaflets 5-9, oblanceolate, copiously hairy on both surfaces, 1-4 cm long. Flowers 6-13 mm long, purplish blue. Lupine was named for the wolf because they were thought at one time to rob the soil. They are now known to fix nitrogen in the soil.

Some species of Lupine are good to eat but others are poisonous and they are hard to tell apart. Those that are most poisonous are worst in the late summer and early fall. At that time the green pods and seeds contain certain alkaloids that can be harmful if eaten in quantity. They are generally considered not terribly harmful after they fully ripen.

Habitat: Dry open ground. Range: British Columbia south to California; east to Montana, Wyoming, and Colorado. Season: May-August.

Silky Lupine
Pea Family (*Leguminosae*)   *Lupinus sericeus*

Name source: *Lupinus* — from the Latin *lupus* which means wolf.

Description: Perennial, branched crown, 2-6 dm tall, appressed-silky. Leaves almost entirely cauline, petiole of lower equal to 3 times length of blades, reduced to equal upward. Leaflets 7-9, oblanceolate, 3-6 cm long, silky on both sides. Flowers 8-12 mm long, upper calyx lip bidentate, lower entire, mostly lavender, rose-colored, or blue, but sometimes yellowish or whitish. Banner well reflexed, silky-hairy on back for about 2/3 length, usually whitish or yellowish centered. Varies more than most *Lupinus* species, albino sporadically, hair and flower vary greatly.

Habitat: Dry ground, hillsides and valleys. Range: British Columbia south to California and Arizona east of Cascades. East to Alberta, Utah, Wyoming, Montana, New Mexico. Season: May-August.

Blue Mountains Prairie Clover, Western Prairie Clover
Pea Family (*Leguminosae*)   *Petalostemon ornatum*

Name source: Greek. *Petalon* — petal; *stemon* — stamen (united petal and stamen); *ornatum* — beautiful, decorative.

Description: Perennial with branches from woody crown, 2-6 dm high. Leaves 3-5 cm. Leaflets 5-7, elliptic to obovate, 1-3 cm long, 3-8 mm broad. Stamens 5. Petals apparently 5, clawed, 1 larger (possibly the only true petal) and attached to base of calyx; other 4 (probably staminodia) attached to short staminal tube, alternate with stamens. Flower pink to rose to purple, blades of "petals" 3-4 mm, claws equal.

Habitat: Rocky or sandy soils. Range: Southeastern Washington (Yakima County) to Lake County, Oregon and western Idaho. Season: June — August.

Least Hop Clover, Shamrock
Pea Family (*Leguminosae*)   *Trifolium dubium*

Name source: *Trifolium* — 3 leaflets; *dubium* — uncertain.

Description: Annual, 1 to several stems, 0.5-5 dm long, prostrate to erect. Petioles shorter than blade. Leaflets 3, cuneate-obovate to obcordate, 5-20 mm long, shallowly denticulate. Stamens 10, pod usually in calyx. Flowers 3-20 in the flower head, pale yellow, 3-4 mm. Banner hoodlike, folded, nearly hiding wings and keel. Considered weed in lawns.

Habitat: Wasteplaces, along roads. Range: Native European weed. Common over United States. Season: April — September.

Large-headed Clover, Big-headed Clover
Pea Family (*Leguminosae*)   *Trifolium macrocephalum*

Name source: *Trifolium* — 3 leaflets; *macrocephalum* — large headed.

Description: Perennial, stem erect, 1-3 dm tall. Lower leaves with long petioles. Leaflets 5-9, rather thick and leathery, oblanceolate to obcordate, 1-2 cm, serrulate. 10-60 flowered. Flowers 2-3 cm long, pinkish to rose-pink to purple, standard often yellowish.

Habitat: Sagebrush desert and Ponderosa pine forests. Range: British Columbia and Idaho to northeastern California and Nevada; eastern Oregon. Season: April — June.

Western Long-spurred Violet, Western Dog Violet
Violet Family (*Violaceae*)   *Viola adunca*

Name source: *Viola* — old Latin name for plant; *adunca* — hooked, bent like a hook.

Description: Perennial, stemless to 20 cm long. Leaf blades 1-3 cm wide, 1-5 cm long, ovate to round-ovate, cordate to cuneate, the margin crenate. Lower petioles slender, 2-8 mm, getting shorter above. Flowers 5-15 mm long, conspicuous spur (½ length of lower petal), blue to violet-blue to deep violet, lower three often whitish based, pencilled with purplish-violet, lateral pair white bearded.

Habitat: Dry to moist meadows, woods, open ground near timberline. Range: Throughout most of western North America, east to Atlantic Coast; from sea level to near timberline. Season: April—August.

Purple Tinged Violet
Violet Family (*Violaceae*)   *Viola purpurea*

Name source: *Viola* — old Latin name for plant; *purpurea* — Latin for purple.

Description: Perennial, stem 5-30 cm high. Leaves 2-4 cm long, petiole 2-6 cm, ovate or orbicular to lanceolate, cuneate to cordate, deeply toothed to subentire. Flowers 5-18 mm broad (petioles 6-8 mm), yellow, brownish-penciled, purple to red to brown on back, the lateral pair bearded.

The young leaves and buds can be used to thicken soup, and for salads and potherbs. The flowers can be candied. The leaves are also used to make tea. Apparently all Viola species are edible.

Habitat: Dry shaded roadside, and cool damp places, lowlands to high in mountains. Range: Chelan County, Washington to California and Arizona; east to Montana, Wyoming, Colorado. Season: April — June.

Common Henbit, Dead Nettle
Mint Family (*Labiatae*)   *Lamium amplexicaule*

Name source: Greek. *Lamium* — meaning throat, from the shape of the flower; *amplexicaule* — stem clasping.

Description: Annual with several weak stems, decumbent below, 1.5-5 dm high. Leaves broadly ovate to nearly orbicular, truncate or cordate base. Lower petioled, 7-10 mm broad, 1.5 cm long. Upper sessile, clasping, 20-25 mm wide, 1.5 cm long. Calyx 5 toothed. Corolla purple or red, 12-18 mm long, tube slender, lower lip with small lateral lobes. Stamens 4. Differs from *L. purpureum* in that all leaves on *L. purpureum* are petiolate.

Habitat: Frequent in fields and waste places. Range: Naturalized from Europe. British Columbia to southern California. Well established in North America. Season: February — October.

61

Mad-dog Skullcap, Narrow-leaved Skullcap
Mint Family (*Labiatae*)   *Scutellaria angustifolia*

Name source: Latin. *Scutella* — tray, refers to appendage of calyx; *angustifolia* — with narrow leaves.

Description: Perennial herb, 1-5 dm tall, erect, often clustered or branched at base. Leaves short petiolate or upper subsessile, blade usually entire, oblong, ovate, 1-4 cm long; lower broader and longer-petioled, often toothed, commonly deciduous. Calyx 3.5-5.5 mm long. Corolla deep blue-violet, 18-28 mm long, tube usually curved, narrow below and dilated above to funnelform throat. Stamens 4. Some members of this genus contain a crystalline glucoside (scutellarin) which is used in cases of nervousness as an antispasmodic.

Habitat: Moist or dry soil, often rocky, in foothills and lowlands. Range: Washington and southern British Columbia to California; chiefly east of the Cascades. East to western and northern Idaho. Season: May — July.

Mullein, Flannel Mullein
Figwort Family (*Scrophulariaceae*)   *Verbascum thapsis*

Name source: *Verbascum* — Latin name for some of the species in this genus.

Description: Tall, robust, leafy stemmed biennial. Leaves densely soft and woolly with branched hairs. The first year a rosette of basal leaves only. The second year a tall alternate leaved flowering stem forms, simple to several-branched, 1-2 m tall. Flowers in long, dense spike-like racemes. Leaves oblanceolate to obovate, entire, the basal 1-4 dm long. Five calyx lobes, lance-ovate. Corolla bright yellow 1.5-2 cm wide. Capsule globular, many seeded. Infusions or smoking of dried leaves used for relieving coughs, throat and lung congestions.

Habitat: Disturbed dry to moist soil. Common on road shoulders. Range: United States and southern Canada. Season: Mid-June to late September.

63

Harsh Indian Paintbrush
Figwort Family (*Scrophulariaceae*)   *Castilleja hispida*

Name source: Named for Domingo Castillejo, Spanish botanist.

Description: Perennial, herbaceous, several stems, 2-6 dm tall, often harsh hairy. Leaves cauline, lanceolate to ovate, usually with 2-3 pairs of lobes, reduced to one in upper, narrower than mid-blade. Bracts and calyces scarlet to orange to yellow. Bracts broad and deeply 3-5 lobed. Calyx 15-30 mm, 4 cleft. Corolla 20-40 mm, elongate and narrow, bilabiate, greenish. Stamens 4. One of the most difficult genera; species limits not clearly defined (150-200 spp.); hybrids. There are several species of red Paintbrushes, known collectively as Indian Paintbrush. It may store selenium.

Habitat: Dry open ground, sagebrush, and open conifer forest. Range: Coastal Oregon and Washington to western Montana and Idaho. Season: Late April—August.

Pallid Paintbrush, Pale Indian Paintbrush
Figwort Family (*Scrophulariaceae*)   *Castilleja pallescens*

Name source: *Castilleja* — Domingo Castillejo, Spanish botanist; *pallescens* — becoming paler in tint.

Description: Perennial, stems clustered, erect or ascending, usually unbranched, 1-2 dm tall. Leaves linear, lower entire, 2-3 cm long, upper with 1-2 pairs of linear divergent lobes. Bracts broader than leaves, 3-5 cleft, yellowish or purplish. Calyx 12-35 mm long. Corolla shorter or a little longer than calyx.

Most of the color on this, and other paintbrushes, comes, not from the flower, but from colored leaves and bracts that surround the flower. Paintbrushes are semi-parasitic. Their roots tap into the roots of other plants to obtain a large part of their nutrients. Pallid Paintbrush is said to have an edible flower.

Habitat: Dry rocky soil, sandy open ground with sagebrush. Range: Northeastern Oregon and northeastern and central Idaho to central and western Wyoming and western and southern Montana. Season: May — August.

Blue-eyed Mary, Blue Lips, Blue Eyes
Figwort Family (*Scrophulariaceae*)   *Collinsia parviflora*

Name source: *Collinsia* — Zacheus Collins, American botanist; *parviflora* — small flower.

Description: Annual. Leaves opposite, usually entire to crenate-dentate, 0.5-4 dm tall. Lower leaves small, petiolate, spatulate to round, commonly deciduous; others sessile, narrowly elliptic or oblong to nearly linear, 5 cm long and 12 mm wide; the upper often whorled. Calyx with 5 sub-equal lobes, 3-6 mm long. Corolla strongly bilabiate, the upper lip 2-lobed, recurved, 4-8 mm; the lower lip 3-lobed, the center lobe shorter. The tube 3-5 mm long, 2-3.5 mm wide. Stamens 4. The seeds generally germinate in the fall, lie dormant through the winter, and grow as soon as it warms up in the spring, there-by getting a jump on other plants.

Habitat: Dry wash. Rocky, gravelly, sandy areas that are moist in spring. Range: Alaska panhandle to southern California. East to Ontario, Michigan, and Colorado. Season: March — July.

Dwarf Monkey-flower, Wild Lettuce
Figwort Family (*Scrophulariaceae*)   *Mimulus nanus*

Name source: *Mimulus* — diminutive of Latin *mimus,* a mimic actor; *nanus* — dwarf.

Description: Annual, dwarf, 1-2 cm tall, becoming much branched. Leaves entire, elliptic-oblanceolate, obtuse, or rounded, 1-3.5 cm long, lower petioled. Calyx 5-8 mm long. Sepals 5, corolla 2-lipped, magenta to purple or, very rarely, yellow, 1-2.5 cm long; throat yellow and deeper red. Stamens 4. The Indians of the area reportedly used the leaves for greens. When raw, they are said to be slightly bitter.

Habitat: Dry talus slope; open, often sandy, or gravelly places, often on pumice. Range: Chelan County, Washington to northern California, east of Cascades; east to southwestern Montana, Yellowstone Park, northeastern Nevada. Season: May — August.

Showy Penstemon
Figwort Family (*Scrophulariaceae*)   *Penstemon speciosus*

Name source: Greek. *Pente* — 5, *stemon* — thread (refers to stamens); *speciosus* — beautifies.

Description: Perennial herbs or shrubs. Leaves opposite, the lower usually petioled. Stamens 4 fertile, 1 infertile. Flowers showy, tubular, bilabiate, typically blue, lavender to pink or red, yellow or white. Many species poorly defined, hybridizes easily, many beautiful native plants. Spaniards of New Mexico boiled flower tops for kidney trouble.

Habitat: Dry rocky ground. Range: Central Washington and eastern Oregon to Utah and California. Season: May – July.

Corn Speedwell
Figwort Family (*Scrophulariaceae*)   *Veronica arvensis*

Name source: Possibly named for St. Veronica.

Description: Annual, erect, 3-30 cm, simple or branched below. Leaves opposite, ovate or broadly elliptic, sometimes subcordate at base, 0.5-1.5 cm long, crenate-serrate, lower generally short-petioled. Corolla blue-violet, 7-7.5 mm wide, nearly rotate, irregularly lobed, upper largest and lower smallest. Stamens 2, exserted.

Habitat: Lawns, gardens, shady fields. Range: From Europe. Season: April—September.

Naked Broomrape, Pale Broomrape, Cancerroot
Broomrape Family (*Orobanchaceae*)   *Orobanche uniflora*

Name source: Greek. *Orobos*—vetch, *anchein*—to choke; *uniflora*—1-flowered.

Description: Stems simple, 0.5-5 dm tall. 1-flowered. Calyx 4-12 mm. Corolla ochroleucous to purple to white, 15-35 mm long. Parasite on roots of many plants, especially Sedum, and various Saxifragaceae, and Compositae. Astringent, applied to ulcers and cancerous growths.

Habitat: Moist or dry places, lowlands to mid-mountain elevations. Range: Mainly east of Cascades from British Columbia to Idaho, California, Montana to Rocky Mountains. Season: March—August.

Desert Plectritis, White Plectritis
Valerian Family (*Valerianaceae*)

Plectritis macrocera

Name source: Greek. *Plektos* — plaited (presumably refers to complex inflorescence), or *plectron* — a spur; *macrocera* — with long horns.

Description: Slender, 1-6 dm tall. Leaves obovate to ovate-lanceolate, reduced upward, petioled below, sessile above, 1-4.5 cm long, entire to serrate. Corolla 5 lobed, 2-6 mm long, white to pinkish with short thick spur, 2 times long as broad, 1.5-2 times tube. Stamens 3. Flower head resembles a small upside-down chandelier. Each little flower is spurred.

Habitat: Dry open ground; vernally moist open places. Range: Southern British Columbia to southern California. East to Montana and Utah. Season: March — June.

71

Common Yarrow, Milfoil, Western Yarrow
Composite Family (*Compositae*)   *Achillea millefolium*

Name source: *Achillea* — for Achilles; *millefolium* — thousand (many) leaves.

Description: Perennial herb. Leaves aromatic, tri-pinnately dissected, the basal petioled, the cauline auriculate and sessile. Heads numerous, radiate, in a flat to round-topped corymbiform panicle, rays 3-8, white, occasionally pink, disk flowers 15-40. Highly variable species.

Achillea was the name of a plant (assumed to be Yarrow) used by Achilles to cure the wounds of his soldiers. The leaves when dried, boiled, and strained are used as a tonic for a run-down feeling or disordered digestion. The plant is also used as a stimulant, aromatic, astringent, diuretic, or vulnerary. When eaten by cattle, it gives milk a bad taste.

Habitat: Dry rocky ground. Range: Common everywhere: roadside, waste ground, disturbed habitats, marshes to semi-desert, coastal bluffs to artic and alpine habitats. Season: April — October.

Pale Agoseris, False Dandelion, Shortbeaked Agoseris
Composite Family (*Compositae*)   *Agoseris glauca*

Name source: Greek. *Aix* — goat, *seris* — chicory; *glauca* — gray covered.

Description: Slender, perennial, 1-7 dm tall. Leaves numerous, linear or lance-linear, 5-35 cm long, entire to little-toothed, sessile. Heads ligulate, yellow, purplish on back.

Habitat: Prairies and lower mountains. Range: East of Cascades in Washington and Oregon. British Columbia to California and Arizona. East to Manitoba and Minnesota. Season: May — September.

Annual Agoseris
Composite Family (*Compositae*)   *Agoseris heterophylla*

Name source: Greek. *Aix* — goat, *seris* — chicory; *heterophylla* — different kinds of leaves.

Description: Slender, erect annual, 3-45 cm tall but usually 6-20 cm, often with several stems from the base. Leaves oblanceolate, toothed or pinnatifid to entire, 4-15 cm long, all in a basal cluster. Heads narrowly campanulate to hemispheric, ligulate, yellow, frequently turning pinkish on drying, 2.5-6 mm long. Involucre 5-13 mm high in flower. The only annual Agoseris.

Habitat: Dry open places, foothills and lowlands. Range: British Columbia to California. East to Idaho, Utah, and Arizona. Season: April — July.

Heart-leaved Arnica
Composite Family (*Compositae*)   *Arnica cordifolia*

Name source: *Arnica* — uncertain, possibly a corruption of *Ptarmica*; *cordifolia* — heart-shaped leaves.

Description: Radiate perennial herb. Stems solitary or few and clustered, 1-3 or sometimes to 7, 1-6 dm tall. Basal leaves long petiolate, cordate; the cauline 2-4 pairs, the lower larger, petiolate with a more or less cordate base, 4-12 cm long. Heads broadly turbinate to campanulate. Involucre 13-20 mm high. Rays 10-15, bright yellow, broad, 1.5-3 cm long, or rarely wanting. Root extract used to soothe sprains and bruises.

Habitat: Mostly in woodlands from foothills to fairly high elevations in mountains. Range: Alaska to New Mexico and California to north Michigan. Rare west of Cascade summit. Season: April — June, rarely to September.

Arrowleaf Balsamroot, Big Sunflower, Bigroot
Composite Family (*Compositae*)   *Balsamorhiza sagittata*

Name source: Greek. *Balsamon* — balsam (resin), *rhiza* — root; *sagittata* — arrowhead shaped.

Description; Perennial herb, 2-8 dm tall. Basal leaves long petiolate, the blade triangular-hastate or with more cordate base, to 2-5 dm long, silvery beneath. Upper leaves reduced. Involucre 1-2 cm wide. Heads solitary, radiate, rays yellow, 2-4 cm, soon deciduous, disk flowers mostly yellow, 8-25 but commonly about 13 or 20.

Most widespread. The Nez Perce Indians cooked the rootstocks on hot stones before eating them. The young stems and leaves can be eaten as a salad. The seeds can be eaten roasted and ground to a flour.

Habitat: Dry open ground, open hillsides and flats. Range: Southern British Columbia to southern California; east of Cascade summit to Montana, South Dakota, and Colorado. Season: April — August.

Serrate Balsam Root
Composite Family (*Compositae*)   *Balsamorhiza serrata*

Name source: Greek. *Balsamon* — balsam (resin), *rhiza* — root; *serrata* — serrate (toothed) leaves.

Description: Perennial with several stems 1-4 dm tall. Leaves green, mostly basal, sometimes 2 reduced on stem, broadly lanceolate or oblong, 4-25 cm long, varying from deltoid-ovate and merely sharp-serrate to evidently pinnatifid, often on same plant, most with some merely toothed. Heads solitary; involucre hemispheric, 18-22 mm high. Rays mostly 10-16, 2-4 cm long.

Habitat: Dry rocky knolls and outcrops. Range: Oregon and southern Washington; east of Cascades. Season: April — June.

Blepharipappus
Composite Family (*Compositae*)

Blepharipappus scaber

Name source: Greek. *Blepharis* — eyelash, *pappus* — seed down, referring to the fringed scales of the pappus; *scaber* — rough to touch.

Description: Annual, 1-3 dm tall. Leaves numerous, 6-30 mm long, to 1.5 mm wide. Involucre turbinate to hemispheric, 4-6 mm high. Heads solitary to numerous, radiate with 2-7 broad white rays. Anthers black. Disk flowers 8-20, 3-cleft, 4-10 mm long, white. Decoction prepared with equal parts milk and water and then cooled, can be used as an application to sore and inflamed eyes.

Habitat: Dry open ground; benchgrass prairies and grassy foothills. Range: Arid regions east of Cascades. Northern California and northwestern Nevada; north to eastern Oregon and adjacent Idaho and southeastern Washington. Season: April — August.

Bachelor's Button, Cornflower
Composite Family (*Compositae*)   *Centaurea cyanus*

Name source: Greek. *Kentaurion*—plant of the Centaurs, name applied to several different genera by herbalists.

Description: Annual, erect, 2-12 dm tall, commonly branched. Leaves basal and lower cauline, oblanceolate or linear-pinnately few-lobed, short petioled, 13 cm long. Flowers blue, varying to white, pink, and purple, the outer flowers much enlarged, the corolla expanded, 16-18 mm long, often unlike the inner in color. The leaves and stem of this plant contain a mild astringent.

Habitat: Dry roadsides, fields, and waste places. Range: Native of Mediterranean, widely established as weed. Cultivated. Season: May—October.

Nevius' Chaenactis, John Day Chaenactis
Composite Family (*Compositae*)   *Chaenactis nevii*

Name source: Greek. *Chaino*—to gape; *akitis*—ray, referring to enlarged and irregular marginal disk corollas of many species.

Description: Annual herb, 1-3 dm, simple or branching from base and midstem. Leaves 2-5 cm, obtusely pinnati-lobate or pinnatifid, the basal greater than the cauline. Heads discoid. Involucre 6-8 mm high. Flowers yellow, regular, funnelform.

Habitat: Dry hillside; heavy clay to volcanic tuff. Range: John Day Valley, Oregon. Season: April—May.

Gold Star, Spring Gold
Composite Family (*Compositae*)   *Crocidium multicaule*

Name source: Greek. *Crocidium* — diminutive derived from *kroke,* loose thread or wool (refers to axillary tomentum); *multicaule* — many stalks.

Description: Delicate annual, generally several-stemmed, to 1.5, or rarely, 3 dm tall. Leaves slightly fleshy, the basal oblanceolate or broader to 2.5 cm, often coarsely few-toothed, the cauline reduced. Heads radiate, yellow; rays 5-13, usually 8, 4-10 mm long, subtended by bracts; disk flowers 1 cm wide or less.

Habitat: Sand plains, cliff ledges, and other dry open places at low elevations. Range: Abundant on sand plains in eastern Oregon and Washington. From Vancouver Island, Puget trough to California; east along and near Columbia River to base of Blue Mountains. North near east base of Cascades to Klickitat County, Washington, and south to northern Deschutes County, Oregon. Season: March — May.

Dwarf Yellow Erigeron, Golden Daisy
Composite Family (*Compositae*)   *Erigeron chrysopsidis*

Name source: Greek. *Eri*—early, *geron*—old man; old man in spring. Early flowering and fruiting.

Description: Perennial, 3-16 cm tall. Leaves all or nearly all in basal cluster, linear-oblanceolate, straight or slightly curved, 3-9 cm long. Heads solitary, hemispheric disk, 11-17 mm wide. Involucre 4-7.5 mm high. Rays yellow, to 10 mm long.

Habitat: Dry open places, often with sagebrush, to 4,000 feet and higher, in Ponderosa pine. Range: Southeastern Washington to northern California; east in Snake River area to Twin Falls, Idaho. Season: May—August.

Slender Rabbit-leaf, Common Hare-leaf
Composite Family (*Compositae*)   *Lagophylla ramosissima*

Name source: Greek. *Lagos* — hare, *phyllon* — leaf (hairy leaves); *ramosissma* — much branched.

Description: Slender, 1-10 dm tall, usually simple to freely branched. Herbage canescent, grayish or dull green. Leaves entire or nearly so, lowermost petioled, oblanceolate or spatulate, 1-10 cm, generally deciduous; others smaller mostly lanceolate to linear or linear-oblong, sessile. Involucre 4.5-8 mm high. Flowers pale yellow, turning purplish or red on lower surface, 1-4 mm long. Ray flowers 5. Disk flowers 6.

Habitat: Damp hillside, dry plains and foothills. Range: Central and eastern Washington and adjacent Idaho to southern Nevada and southern California. Season: May — August.

Butterweed, Tall Western Senecio
Composite Family (*Compositae*)   *Senecio integerrimus*

Name source: Latin. *Senex* — an old man (probably referring to the white pappus or the pubescence of some species); *integerrimus* — smooth edge.

Description: Perennial, stem arising singly, 3-10 dm. Leaves basal and lower cauline, ovate to oblong or lanceolate, entire, dentate or denticulate, narrowed to subcordate at base, blade thickish, 6-25 cm long-petioled; upper smaller, reduced to bracts at or below the middle. Heads several. Involucre 5-10 mm high. Rays 5-10, 6-15 mm, yellow.

Poisonous: cattle and horses most sensitive, sheep and goats maybe half as much. The effects are cumulative; symptoms may not appear until after months of liver damage, or they may appear abruptly in horses. Symptoms include a sweetish unpleasant odor from the skin, weakness, uneasiness, abdominal pain, emaciation, reduced sensibility. They may chew on mangers, fences, dirt. They may die quietly, or start walking aimlessly through or into anything. In people, symptoms of poisoning include ascites, enlarged liver, abdominal pain, nausea, vomiting, headache, apathy, emaciation, maybe diarrhea, vomitus with blood. These toxins are not destroyed in drying.

Habitat: Moderately dry to moist places in open woods, valleys to timberline. Range: Chiefly east of Cascades from southern British Columbia; east to Saskatchewan and Minnesota. Season: May — July.

Dandelion
Composite Family (*Compositae*)   *Taraxacum officinale*

Name source: Uncertain, possibly Greek. *Tarassein*—to stir up (referring to medical properties); *officinale*—of practical use to man.

Description: Perennial, 5-50 cm high. Leaves oblong-spatulate, runcinate-pinnatifid, or lobed pinnatifid, dentate, or rarely nearly entire, usually with large terminal lobe, 6-40 cm. Heads solitary, 2.5-5 cm broad. Flowers all ligulate, numerous, yellow.

For centuries the root has been used as a tonic, diuretic, and mild laxative. Many people cook the leaves as greens, use the roots in salads and use the flowers in making wine. Some people have been known to cook the flowers into pancakes. The seeds are also edible.

Habitat: Open fields, roadsides, lawns. Range: Widespread. Native of Europe and Asia. Season: May—October.

85

Showy Townsendia
Composite Family (*Compositae*)   *Townsendia florifer*

Name source: *Townsendia* — David Townsend, botanist 1789-1858; *florifer* — flower bearing.

Description: Low depressed branching biennial, 5-16 cm in diameter. Leaves spatulate, pubescent, 2-5 cm long. Heads radiate, numerous and large. Involucre campanulate, 8-10 mm high. Rays 15-30, pink, lavender, cream or white, 9-12 mm long.

Habitat: Sagebrush region. Range: East side of Cascades and adjacent plateaus to Montana, Utah, and Nevada. Season: May — July.

Meadow Salsify, Yellow Goatsbeard, Oysterplant
Composite Family (*Compositae*)   *Tragopogon dubius*

Name source: Greek. *Tragos* — goat, *pogon* — beard.

Description: Biennial or annual, 3-10 dm tall, rather bushy. Leaves linear-lanceolate, 12-15 cm long. Heads ligulate, yellow. Involucral bracts long, about 13.

Salsify was cultivated in Europe and introduced by the early colonists, and was soon used by the Indians as food. The cooked roots supposedly taste like oysters or parsnips, depending on whom you talk to. The juice is used as a cure for indigestion and mixed with woman's milk, it is reputed to be a cure-all for disorders of the eye.

Habitat: Dry ground; fields and waste places that are rather open and dry. Range: Introduced from Europe. Southwestern Washington and adjacent Idaho; south and east to Arizona and Texas. Season: May — September.

Vegetable oyster
Composite Family (*Compositae*)   *Tragopogon porrifolius*

Name source: Greek. *Tragos* — goat, *pogon* — beard.

Description: All species of *Tragopogon* are introduced-escaped biennial or perennial herbs with a milky sap and a taproot. Leaves alternate, entire, linear, clasping. Leaves of *porrifolius* glabrous with heads of purple ligulate florets. Fruits form dandelion-like sphere of bristles.

These species have a milky sap which has been used for various medicinal purposes and for chewing gum. The peeled root can be eaten raw or cooked, and is said by some to taste like oysters.

Habitat: Moist places. Range: Old World native. Naturalized as weed in Pacific States. Season: April — August (November).

Heart-leaved Eriogonum, Composite Eriogonum
Buckwheat Family (*Polygonaceae*)   *Eriogonum compositum*

Name source: Greek. *Erion* — wool, *gony* — knee.

Description: Perennial with a deep woody root and a few-branched crown. Leaves all basal, ovate, cordate base, long petiole, white tomentose below, thin tomentose to glabrous above, 7-25 cm by 1.5-5 cm. Flowering stems 2-5 dm tall, compound umbel, linear to oblong bracts, yellow or white, sometimes turning to rose. Headache and stomachache remedy; good honey.

Habitat: On tables, rimrock, cliffs to open rocky dry ground. Range: East of Cascades, Chelan County, Washington, Northern California, Idaho and Nez Perce Counties, Idaho. Season: May — July.

Hornseed Buttercup

Buttercup Family (*Ranunculaceae*)   *Ranunculus testiculatus*

Name source: *Testiculatus* — having two oblong tubercles.

Description: Leaves all basal, 1.5-4 cm, ternate to biternate. Flower 2-8 cm tall. Sepals greenish, ovate, lanceolate, 1-6 mm long. Petals yellow, 5-8 mm long, narrow. Stamens 10-15. Forms dry, hard burr (fruit). Many species of buttercup or crowfoot (Ranunculus) were used externally for various medicinal purposes, and all are poisonous when eaten raw.

Habitat: Sagebrush desert, and often common on road shoulders. Range: Recently introduced Furasian species, spread rapidly through Northwest east of Cascades, eastern Washington and Oregon to Nevada, Idaho, and Colorado. Season: March—May.

Sage Buttercup, Crowfoot, Early Buttercup
Buttercup Family (*Ranunculaceae*)   *Ranunculus glaberrimus*

Name source: *Ranunculus* — little frog; *glaberrimus* — smoothest, very smooth, bare.

Description: Perennial. Leaves mostly basal, orbicular, elliptic, ovate to obovate, entire to 3-lobed to 3-parted, long petiole. Sepals 5, usually purple-tinged, 5-8 mm long. Petals 5, yellow, 4-5 mm long, broadly ovate. Stamens several, 4-20 cm long.

Buttercups as a group tend to be somewhat poisonous; this one is mildly poisonous. May cause poisoning similar to Delphinium. In general posesses an acrid juice in stem and leaves that blisters mouths of cattle. European beggars rub skin with juice to imitate sores. Ancients used it to remove birthmarks and as a last resort to cure leprosy. Indians ground parched seeds with others to make flour with the flavor of parched corn that is eaten raw, the bitter taste gone.

Habitat: Damp meadow, sandy soil, sagebrush deserts, and Ponderosa pine forests. Range: British Columbia to Plumas County, California, east to Colorado, Dakotas, Nebraska, and New Mexico. Season: April — early June.

Small Alyssum, Yellow Alyssum
Mustard Family (*Cruciferae*)   *Alyssum alyssoides*

Name source: Greek. *A* — not or without; *lyssa* — madness. Believed of value in controlling anger, madness, hydrophobia.

Description: Stem branched from base, gray, hairy, 6-30 cm tall. Leaves narrowly oblanceolate, spatulate, entire, 5-25 mm long. Sepals 2 mm, persistent until fruit is nearly mature. Petals cream or white, narrow, 2-4 mm long. Believed to have value in allaying anger, and madness.

Habitat: Dry, sandy soil. Range: Wasteland and roadsides throughout United States. From Europe. Season: April — July.

Blind-weed, Caseweed, Lady's Purse, Mother's Heart, Pepper and Shot, Pickpocket, Witches Pouch
Mustard Family (*Cruciferae*)   *Capsella bursa-pastoris*

Name source: *Capella* — Latin for a little box, referring to the silicle-seal.

Description: Annual herb. 1-5 dm tall, simple or branched. Basal leaves lanceolate to oblong, dentate to pinnatifid forming rosette, 5-12 cm. Stem leaves sagittate-clasping. Seed coat mucilaginous when wet. Petals white or pale yellow. Has been sold as an astringent in eastern United States. Pods used for flavor, dried. Young leaves eaten raw and for greens (blanched). Roots used as a substitute for ginger and candied by boiling in rich sugar syrup. Potherb.

Habitat: Wasteplaces, roadsides, gardens, even subalpine. Range: Weed throughout most of North America; introduced from Europe. Season: March—July.

Hoary Cress
Mustard Family (*Cruciferae*)   *Cardaria draba*

Name source: Greek. *Kardia* — heart, shape of silicles in some species.

Description: Hoary, pubescent. Stems erect to decumbent, 2-5 dm high, branching at top. Leaves oblong to ovate, entire or dentate, 3-10 cm long, the lower petioled, the upper clasping. Petals white.

Habitat: Widely distributed in old fields, roadsides. Range: Native of Europe, spread over much of western United States. Season: April — August.

Yellow Tansy-Mustard, Hedge Mustard, Plixweed
Mustard Family (*Cruciferae*)   *Descurainia pinnata*

Name source: *Pinnata* — pinnate leaves.

Description: Annual herb, 1-7 dm tall. Leaves mainly cauline, broadly lanceolate to oblanceo-late, lower ones petiolate, 3-10 cm, bipinnate-pinnatifid to (commonly) pinnate-pinnatifid and somewhat toothed. Upper leaves reduced. Sepals 1-2 mm. Petals pale to bright yellow, 1.5-3.5 mm long. Siliques 4-20 mm long. When eaten in large quantities by cattle during early spring blooming D. pinnata can cause blindness, inability to swallow and death. It can be eaten as a green or the seeds can be eaten parched and ground.

Habitat: Dry ground. Range: Widespread and extremely variable; in most of United States and Canada. Season: April — July.

Vernal Whitlow-grass, Draba
Mustard Family (*Cruciferae*)   *Draba verna*

Name source: *Draba* — from Dioscorides who first used *drabe*, meaning acrid, for some member of *Cruciferae; verna* — spring.

Description: Annual, 5-20 cm high. Leaves all in a basal rosette, spatulate to oblanceolate, entire or with a few coarse teeth, 5-25 mm long. Petals white, deeply bilobed, 2-4 mm long. Introduced from Europe.

Habitat: Dry open ground, open grassy plains to sagebrush desert or lower mountains. Range: Throughout much of United States and Canada. Season: February — May.

Bushy Wallflower, Repand Wallflower
Mustard Family (*Cruciferae*)   *Erysimum repandum*

Name source: *Erysimum*—Greek, *erusimon* from *eryo* (to draw); *repandum*—with slightly uneven margin.

Description: Annual 2-5 dm tall, simple to (usually) freely branched. Leaves lanceolate to oblanceolate, up to 15 cm long and 12 mm broad, usually sinuate-dentate to repand-lobate, sometimes subentire. Petals light yellow, 6-9 mm long. Introduced from Europe.

Habitat: Talus slope; desert plains and lower mountains. Range: Eastern Oregon and Washington to central California, scattered east to Atlantic Coast. Season: April—June.

Pale Wallflower, Western Wallflower
Mustard Family (*Cruciferae*)   *Erysimum occidentale*

Name source: *Erysimum*— Greek, *erusimon; occidentale*— western.

Description: Biennial, usually unbranched, 1-8 dm tall. Basal leaves many in a rosette, linear-oblanceolate, 4-8 cm long, mostly entire, sometimes with a few teeth. Stem leaves linear to linear-lanceolate, 1-3 mm broad, usually entire. Sepals 7-10 mm long. Petals bright yellow with an obovate blade, 6-10 mm long.

Habitat: Sagebrush hills and valleys. Range: Southeastern Washington to eastern Oregon to Idaho and Nevada. Season: March—July.

Yellow-flowered Peppergrass, Roundleaved Peppergrass, Clasping Peppergrass
Mustard Family (*Cruciferae*)   *Lepidum perfoliatum*

Name source: Greek. *Lepis* — scale ("scalelike" silicles); *perfoliatum* — stem passing through leaf.

Description: Branched annual, stem 2-6 dm tall. Basal leaves bi- or tri-pinnately divided into linear segments. Lower cauline simple changing to cordate-clasping, ovate-denticulate to (usually) entire. Petals tiny, yellow, 1.5 mm long. Can be eaten as a garnish or salad.

Habitat: Dry, open ground. Range: Well established European weed; dry, waste, or over-grazed land. Introduced from Europe. Season: March — June.

Western Bladderpod, Western Lesquerella
Mustard Family (*Cruciferae*)   *Lesquerella occidentalis*

Name source: *Lesquerella* — Leo Lesquereux (1805-1889), American bryologist; *occidentalis* — western.

Description: Silvery, biennial or perennial. Stems usually simple, several, prostrate to erect, 5-20 cm long. Basal leaves many, forming a rosette, 1.5-8 cm long, the blade ovate to oblance-olate, obovate, 5-22 mm broad, entire to repand, tapered uniformly to the petiole. Cauline leaves mostly 1-5, oblanceolate, usually entire, 5-15 mm. Petals yellow, 7-10 mm.

Habitat: Rocky hillsides. Range: Northeastern Oregon to California, central Idaho, Utah. Season: May — July.

Tumbling Mustard, Jim Hill Mustard
Mustard Family (*Cruciferae*)   *Sisymbrium altissimum*

Name source: *Sisymbrium*—Latinized Greek for some member of *Cruciferae*, possibly watercress; *altissimum*—very high.

Description: Bushy-branched annual, 3-15 dm tall. Basal leaves 8-20 cm long, oblong, oblanceolate, lanceolate. Lower ones pinnatifid, petioled becoming pinnatifid into linear segments. Upper ones reduced in size, sessile. Petals pale yellow, 5-8 mm long. Sepals 4 mm long. Potherb. Young leaves and shoots occasionally used as salad. Foliage reported poisonous to livestock. Seeds gathered and eaten in soup and gruel.

Habitat: Mostly in waste places. Range: From Europe. Widespread. Washington To California, especially east of Cascades. Season: May—September.

101

Golden Cleome, Bee Plant, Stinkweed, Spiderflower, Broad-podded Cleome
Caper Family (*Capparidaceae*)   *Cleome platycarpa*

Name source: *Cleome* — name used by Theophrastus for mustard-like plant; *platycarpa* — bearing broad fruit.

Description: Annual 1-7 dm tall, simple or branched. Leaves 3-foliolate, oval to lanceolate or oblanceolate, entire, 1-3 cm long, petiole longer than the blade. Petals ovate, deep yellow to orange, 5-8 mm long. Stamens 6, very long, two times the length of the petals.

The boiled leaves and flowers can be eaten as greens. A large quantity boiled down makes a black dye. Important food for Indians: young shoots used as potherb, boiled shoots rolled into balls and stored for later use.

Habitat: Dry roadside. Alkaline and lava soils, light and sandy to heavy clays (especially heavy clays of John Day Valley in Oregon). Range: Eastern Oregon to northeastern California, Idaho, Nevada. Season: May — August.

Slender Cinquefoil
Rose Family (*Rosaceae*)   *Potentilla gracilis*

Name source: *Potentilla* — from the Latin *potens*, powerful — the supposed medicinal properties of some species; *gracilis* — graceful.

Description: Stems erect to ascending, 4-8 dm tall. Basal leaves numerous, long-petioled, to 3 dm, several leaflets (5-9) cuneate-oblanceolate to broadly oblanceolate or oblong-elliptic, 3-8 cm long, from evenly crenate-dentate to deeply dissected almost to the midvein, 5-6 + cm wide, lower side often fine white-hairy (tomentose). Stem leaves 1-2. Calyx 6-10 mm broad, the 5 lobes 4 by 10 mm. Petals yellow, obovate-obcordate, slightly to considerably longer than sepals, often greater than 1 cm. Stamens usually 20. Pistils numerous. An extremely variable, diverse plant. The root is probably edible as roots of similar plants are, either raw or cooked.

Habitat: Wet meadow; moist places, often saline soil, sagebrush desert, subalpine meadows. Range: Alaska south to northern California and Sierra Nevada to Baja; east to Saskatchewan, Dakotas, Nebraska, New Mexico, and Arizona. Season: May — August.

103

White-stemmed Mentzelia
Loasa Family (*Loasaceae*)   *Mentzelia albicaulis*

Name source: *Mentzelia* — C. Mentzel (1622-1701), German botanist; *albicaulis* — white stalk.

Description: Annual, simple to freely branched, 1-4 dm tall with white stems. Leaves 2-10 cm long, the basal petioled, narrowly oblong or lanceolate, from nearly entire to deeply pin-natifid with linear lobes. Calyx 1-2 cm, the lobes 2-4 mm. Petals golden yellow, often copper-colored at base, 2-6 mm. Stamens 15-35. This plant has the ability to absorb and store selenium from the soil. It generally grows in Cretaceous and Eocene shales.

Habitat: Dry sandy or rocky soil in desert valleys and foothills. Range: British Columbia to California; mostly east of Cascades and Sierra Nevada. East to Montana and New Mexico. Season: May — July.

Brittle Prickly Pear, Indian Fig
Cactus Family (*Cactaceae*)   *Opuntia fragilis*

Name source: *Opuntia* — apparently named for Greek town; *fragilis* — brittle.

Description: Low mats, 0.5-2 dm tall. Stem joints not greatly flattened, ovoid to terete or moderately compressed, 2-5 (lower to 10) cm long, the upper easily detached. Spines 2-7, straight, yellowish-brownish, 1-4 cm long with many short barbed woolly stickers. Flowers 3-5 cm long, yellow.

The fruit is edible cooked or raw and can be boiled down to a syrup. A bitter juice can be crushed from the pads that quenches thirst. Indians used the pads split and soaked in water to bind wounds and bruises. In Mexico the pads are boiled and crushed, and the sticky juice is added to whitewash and mortar to make it stick better. The pulp is edible; the fruit can be dried or used for jelly; the seeds can be dried and stored.

Habitat: Dry hillsides and open ground. Range: East of Cascades from British Columbia to northern California. East to Texas, Wisconsin, Arizona. Season: May-July.

Lomatium, Desert Parsley, Biscuitroot
Parsley Family (*Umbelliferae*)   *Lomatium Spp.*

Name source: Greek. *Loma*— a border, refers to winged fruit.

Description: Species so variable that a good key is hard to devise. About 75 species in western and central North America. Low, short-stemmed perennial herbs. Roots fleshy, tuber-like. Leaves mainly basal, ternately or pinnately compound, often dissected. Umbels compound. Sepals small. Petals yellow, white, pink, or purplish. Lomatiums are very similar and notoriously difficult to impossible to tell apart without a mature seed. Even then they are not easy. To make matters worse, they tend to cross-pollinate and hybridize. They can normally be eaten as greens. The thick roots were food for Indians.

Habitat: Open areas. Range: Western and central America.

Large-flowered Collomia
Phlox Family (*Polemoniaceae*)   *Collomia grandiflora*

Name source: *Collomia* — kolla, meaning glue; *grandiflora* — large flower.

Description: Annual. Stem simple to branched, 1-10 dm tall. Leaves linear or lanceolate, occasionally elliptic, entire, sessile, numerous, 4-10 cm long. Calyx lobes to 8 mm. Corolla salmon or yellowish to nearly white, narrowly funnelform, 2-3 times calyx, 1.5-3 cm long, lobes lanceolate 5-7 mm. The outer covering of the seeds contains an unusually large amount of mucus which diffuses like a smoke cloud when the seed is dropped into water.

Habitat: Dry open ground to sparsely wooded areas. Range: West of Rockies, both sides of Cascades from northern Washington and adjacent British Columbia to California and Arizona. Season: May — August.

Common Fiddleneck, Tarweed
Borage Family (*Boraginaceae*)   *Amsinckia intermedia*

Name source: *Amsinckia* — William Amsinck, patron of Hamburg Botanic Center, early 19th century; *intermedia* — between (other species?).

Description: Coarse bristly annual herb. Simple to much branched, 2-9 dm tall. Leaves mostly broadly linear to oblong or lanceolate, up to 15 cm long and 2 cm wide. Sepals free, 6-12 mm long in fruit. Corolla 7-10 mm long, funnelform or salverform, orange or orange-yellow with vermillion throat, well above calyx, limb 4-6 mm wide. Extremely variable, of wide developmental range, may interbreed with other species. Species very much alike. The seeds of fiddlenecks are poisonous to cattle, horses, and swine, but apparently not to sheep, mules, fowl. Acts as a liver toxin; liver becomes small, hard, and less and less functional.

Habitat: Dry ground, grassy hills, and valleys. Range: Washington and Oregon east and west sides of Cascades, to Idaho. South to southern Arizona, southern California, and Mexican Baja. Season: April—May.

Cryptantha
Borage Family (*Boraginaceae*)   *Cryptantha (probably flaccida)*

Name source: Greek. *Kryptos* — hidden, *anthos* — flower.

Description: Low, erect or branching annual or perennial herbs. Leaves mostly narrow, alternate. Flowers on sympodial helicoid false spikes. Calyx 5 parted. Corolla 5-lobed, usually white, small, often minute, funnelform or salverform, throat partially closed by 5 often yellow fornices. Some species have cleistogamous flowers with fertilization occuring inside the closed flower.

Habitat: Dry open ground. Range: Central and southeastern Washington to southern California and along western fringe of Idaho. Season: May — June (*flaccida*).

Cleaver wort, Cleavers, Goosegrass, Bedstraw, Turkey-grass
Madder Family (*Rubiaceae*)   *Galium aparine*

Name source: *Gala* — milk; *aparine* — bedstraw (clinging, holding on).

Description: Annual. Square stems weak, usually scrambling over bushes, 1-15 dm high, sometimes erect, seldom much branched. Leaves in whorls of 4-8, linear to narrowly lanceolate or oblanceolate, 1-5 cm long. Corolla rotate, 4-parted, greenish-white, 1-2 mm wide. Stamens 4 or 5. Diurdic, refrigerant — used by Indians for fevers and inflammations.

Habitat: Common weedy species, edges of thickets and open woodland. Range: Wide distribution in United States, Europe, and Asia. Season: April — August.

Bitterroot, Resurrection Flower
Purslane Family (*Portulacaceae*)   *Lewisia rediviva*

Name source: *Lewisia* — for Meriwether Lewis. *Rediviva* — refers to the plant's ability to return to vigor after the root has been dried for weeks or even months.

Description: Stems 1-flowered, 1-3 cm high. Leaves basal, 1.5-5 cm long, fleshy, nearly round, usually withering before flowering. Bracts 5-8, scarious, linear, joint just above bracts falls off. Sepals 4-9, oval, 10-25 mm long, unequal, whitish to rose, entire. Petals 12-18, white to pink to rose, 15-30 mm long. Stamens 30-50. Varies in color and size; Rocky Mountain versions tend to be redder.

The roots of Bitterroot were collected in large quantities by Indians. They were generally collected in the spring before the stored starch had been used by the developing flower. Raw, the roots have a bitter taste, hence the name, but boiled or baked with the outer covering peeled off they are rather tasty. They are a good source of concentrated nutrition; best eaten in the spring. The pounded dry root is used for sore throat.

Habitat: Dry, rocky hilltop. Rocky, sterile soil. Range: East of Cascades. British Columbia to southern California; east to Montana, Colorado, Arizona. Season: March — July.

111

Miner's Lettuce, Indian Lettuce, Spanish Lettuce
Purslane Family (*Portulacaceae*)   *Montia perfoliata*

Name source: *Perfoliata* — leaf through stem.

Description: Very variable, 5-40 cm high, with many branches. Basal leaves rhombic, ovate, linear, up to 3 cm broad, 1 cm long, petioles may be as long as stems. Two stem leaves joined together in a disk .6-5 cm broad. Sepals 1.5-5 cm, ovate, orbicular. Petals 5, white to pink, from slightly longer to twice length of sepals. Stamens 5. Widely used by early settlers as a salad green. Also said to avert and cure scurvy. Tea made from leaves is a laxative.

Habitat: Wet stream bank, moist shady ground. Range: British Columbia to Baja California, both sides of Cascades, east to Dakotas, Wyoming, Utah, Arizona. Season: February — July.

Spring Beauty, Siberian Montia, Candy Flower
Purslane Family (*Portulacaceae*)   *Montia sibirica*

Name source: *Montia*—for Italian Botanist, Guiseppe Monti, 1682-1760; *sibirica*—of Siberian origin.

Description: Stems 1-5 dm high, usually several. Basal leaves elliptic to rhombic-ovate, blades 1-7 cm long, petioles 2-3 times length of blades. Stem leaves 2, opposite, sessile to short-petioled, 1-5 cm broad, up to 7 cm long, lanceolate to ovate-rhombic. Calyx 2.5-6 cm. Petals 5, white to deep pink, white with pink lines, 6-12 mm long, deeply notched.

Habitat: Moist shady places, lowlands to mid-elevations. Range: Siberia to Alaska, south to southern California on both sides of Cascades, east to Montana and Utah. Season: March—September.

Pale Montia, Common Montia
Purslane Family (*Portulacaceae*)   *Montia spathulata*

Name source: *Montia* — for Italian Botanist, Guiseppe Monti, (1682-1760).

Description: Stems several, simple, 2-10 cm high. Basal leaves linear or linear-spatulate, generally longer than stems, numerous. Stem leaves 2, opposite, linear-lanceolate, 5-10 mm long, united on one or both sides, joined at base. Sepals 1-2 mm. Petals white to pink, distinct, 2.5-4.5 mm, notched or rounded. Stamens 5. Variable.

Habitat: Dry to moist soil, open grass, gravelly to sandy. Range: British Columbia south to central or southern California coast, west of Cascades to Utah, Colorado River. Both sides of Cascades in Oregon. Season: February—May.

Jagged Chickweed
Pink Family (*Caryophyllaceae*)   *Holosteum umbellatum*

Name source: Greek. *Holo*—whole or all; *osteon*—bone (apparently inappropriate and possibly humorous reference to frailty of plant); *umbellatum*—having umbel.

Description: Annual, branched at base, 5-25 cm high, glandular-pubescent above. Basal leaves oblanceolate, stem leaves oblong, sessile to short-petioled, 1-3.5 cm long. Umbels 3-16. Sepals distinct, 2.5-5 mm long, petals slightly exceeding the sepals. Introduced from Europe.

Habitat: Dry open ground. Range: Europe and northeast Asia. Sparingly established in northeast Oregon, eastern Washington, and adjacent Idaho. Mostly along Colorado and Snake Rivers. Season: April—May.

Rockcress
Mustard Family (*Cruciferae*) 　　　　　　　　　　　　　　　　　*Genus Arabis*

Name source: *Arabis* — for Arabia.

Description: Annual to perennial herbs, rarely shrubby. Basal leaves entire to lyrate-pinnatifid. Stem leaves usually auriculate, alternate. Petals white to pink to red purple, obovate-spatulate siliques linear. Extremely difficult to distinguish species, very variable. Most important characteristics are of mature fruit and seeds. Some would fit into rock gardens of dry areas, do not tolerate moisture.

Habitat: Desert to alpine areas. Range: More than 100 species found in Northern Hemisphere.

African Malcolmia
Mustard Family (*Cruciferae*)   *Malcolmia africana*

Name source: *Malcolmia* — for William Malcolm (1778-1805), British horticulturist.

Description: Stem branched from base, 1.5-4 dm tall. Leaves simple, many, lanceolate to elliptic-lanceolate, 3-10 cm long (including petiole), remotely sharply dentate, the upper reduced. Sepals 3-4 mm. Petals rose to purple with darker veins, 6-8 mm. Malcolmia has a very strong, somewhat unpleasant odor. It can grow in such profusion as to turn fields purple. It has been introduced in this country from northern Africa.

Habitat: Dry open ground. Range: Spreading through the western United States. Season: April — June.

117

Watercress
Mustard Family (*Cruciferae*)   *Rorippa nasturtium-aquaticum*

Name source: *Rorippa*—from Saxon name for plant, *rorippen*; *aquaticum*—living in water.

Description: Stems floating, 1-6 dm long. Leaves compound with 3-11 leaflets. Leaflets ovate to lanceolate, the uppermost usually largest. Petals broadly spatulate, white to purple, veined or tinted, 3-4 mm long. The leaves and young stems of watercress are widely used in salads and garnishes. In Europe it is raised and sold commercially. The Romans considered it good for people with deranged minds.

Habitat: Pine Creek; slow moving water. Range: Well established in North America. Season: March—October.

Alum root
Saxifrage Family (*Saxifragaceae*)   *Heuchera grossulariifolia*

Name source: Named for Johann Heinrich von Heucher, (1677-1747) Professor of Medicine at Wittenberg.

Description: Flowering stems, leafless, 1.5-6.5 dm tall. Leaf blades cordate-orbicular to cordate-reniform, 1-7 cm broad, 5-7 lobed for 1/5 to 1/3 length, lobes 2-3 times crenate-dentate. Petiole 3-7 cm long. Calyx 4-6 mm long. Petals white, from shorter than sepals to 1.5 times length. Stamens shorter than sepals. Raw roots of this plant have been believed to cure diarrhea.

Habitat: Rock face. Grass hillsides and rocky canyon walls to alpine scree and talus slopes. Range: Southwestern Montana and central Idaho to eastern Oregon. Season: May— early August.

Small-flowered Fringe-cup, Star-flower, Prairie Star, Woodland Star
Saxifrage Family (*Saxifragaceae*)   *Lithophragma parviflora*

Name source: Greek. *Lithos* — stone; *phragma* — wall, supposed reference to habitat of plant; *parviflora* — small flower.

Description: 1-5 dm tall. Basal leaves petioled, 2-6 cm, blades 3-5 parted, 1-3 cm broad and once or twice 3-cleft. Stem leaves 2-3, often divided and sessile. Petals 5, white to pink or purple, fringed, 3-5 lobed, 4-12 mm. Calyx 5-lobed, 4-6 mm. Stamens 10. This is one of the early blooming flowers. The earlier blossoms are usually pinkish, turning lighter as the season progresses. Fits in rock garden but has short season.

Habitat: Dry wash. Prairies and grassland to sagebrush desert, rocky and gravelly ground. Range: British Columbia south to northern California, east to Alberta and South Dakota, south to Colorado. Season: March — June.

Broad-petaled Strawberry
Rose Family (*Rosaceae*)   *Fragaria virginiana*

Name source: *Fragaria* — from *fraga,* Latin name for strawberry; *fragum* — fragrance.

Description: Leaves long petioled, to 15 cm, 3 leaflets, each broadly obovate or cuneate-obovate to elliptic-obovate, 2-5 cm long, coarsely crenate-serrate most of length. Stolonous stems, peduncles shorter than to sometimes as long as the leaf. Petals 5, white, 6-13 mm long, orbicular. Sepals 5. Stamens 20. Fruit 10-14 mm in diameter. Wild Strawberries taste great; most people say even better than cultivated ones. Indians made a tea from the leaves.

Habitat: Moist stream banks and sandy or gravelly meadows to open woods. Range: Alaska to California, east to Colorado, Montana, and New Mexico. Season: May — August.

121

Filaree, Stork's Bill, Red-stemmed Filaree, Cranes-bill, Clocks, Alfilaria
Geranium Family (*Geraniaceae*)   *Erodium cicutarium*

Name source: Greek. *Erodium—erodios,* a heron, reference to long beak; *circutarium—* resembling water hemlock or cow bone, *Cicuta.*

Description: Annual, 0.3-5 dm tall. Leaves mostly basal, rosulate, pinnate-pinnatifid to pinnately divided and segments incised, ultimate divisions very narrow. Stem reddish. Flowers pinkish to purple. Sepals 4-8 mm long. Petals a little longer. Stamens 10, 5 with anthers.

The seeds of this plant germinate in the fall, giving it a jump on the other flowers of the area. A palatable and nutritious plant, it is valuable as stock feed, especially for sheep. It can also be eaten as greens either raw or cooked. The plant is also an astringent and diuretic. It may occasionally store dangerous quantities of nitrates. Variable species.

Habitat: Dry open ground, drier plains and hillsides. Range: Western United States. Introduced from Europe. Season: February—July.

Wild Geranium, Sticky Geranium, Crane's Bill
Geranium Family (*Geraniaceae*)   *Geranium viscosissimum*

Name source: Greek. *Geranos* — crane, long beak; *viscosissimum* — sticky.

Description: Perennial with stout stems, 3-9 dm tall. The stem and leaves are covered with small sticky hairs. Leaf blades 5-12 mm broad, 5-7-parted to 3/4 length, divisions obovate-cuneate, sharply toothed. Petioles 2-4 dm long. Sepals 5, 8-12 mm. Petals 5, 10-20 mm long, rounded, pinkish-lavender to purple with dark veins. Stamens 10.

Habitat: Moist meadows, lowlands to well into mountains. Range: British Columbia to northern California east of Cascades, east to Saskatchewan, south to western South Dakota, Colorado, Utah, Nevada. Season: May — August.

123

Western Blue Flax, Prairie Flax
Flax Family (*Linaceae*)   *Linum perenne*

Name source: *Linum* — Latin name for flax.

Description: Perennial, 1-6 dm, often branched at base. Leaves alternate, linear, 1-5 cm long. Sepals 4-7 mm. Petals blue, rarely white, obovate, 10-23 mm long.

Fiber used for string. The seeds are edible when cooked; raw they may cause problems. In medicine the plant serves as a laxative. Stems were steeped for stomach disorders. Poultices of crushed fresh leaves were used for swelling. Early settlers made poultices of powdered seeds, corn, and boiling water mixed in paste for infected wounds and mumps.

Habitat: Dry ground, prairies to alpine ridges, mountain meadows and grassy slopes, dry well-drained soil. Range: Western North America. Season: May — July.

124

White-leaved Globe Mallow, Desert Mallow, Currant-leaved Desert Mallow,
Red Globe Mallow
Mallow Family (*Malvaceae*)   *Sphaeralcea munroana*

Name source: Greek. *Spaera* — sphere, *alcea* — mallow, referring to globose fruits.

Description: Perennial, grayish, hairy, 2-8 dm tall. Leaf blades 2-6 cm long, ovate deltoid; cleft in leaves. Calyx 5-10 mm. Petals apricot-pink to reddish. This family's distinctive characteristics are redder flowers and cleft in leaves.

Habitat: Open sagebrush desert to lower mountain elevations and dry roadsides. Range: California to western Montana, Colorado, Nevada; north to south central British Columbia. Season: May — August.

Shortseeded Waterwort
Waterwort Family (*Elatinaceae*)   *Elatine brachysperma*

Name source: Greek. *Elatine* — fir-like red leaves; *brachysperma* — short seeds.

Description: Stems prostrate, 2-5 cm. Leaves oblong or oval to lanceolate, 2-6 mm long. Flowers minute. Petals and sepals 2-3, pinkish.

Habitat: Margins of ponds; grows in mud or sometimes submerged. Range: Eastern Washington and Oregon to coast ranges of central and southern California. East to Ohio. Season: April — May.

126

Hedgehog-thistle
Cactus Family (*Cactaceae*)   *Pediocactus simpsonii*

Name source: Greek. *Pedion* — field.

Description: Stems depressed globose, single to clustered, 7-25 cm thick. Central spines 8-12, 8-25 mm long, yellowish to reddish brown with a dark lip. Marginal spines 10-30, shorter, whiter. Flowers 1.5-3.5 cm long, yellowish-green to purple. The fruit and core of this cactus are probably edible. Pack-rats can pull off clumps of spines to eat out the juicy center. They have also been known to use the spines to protect their nests.

Habitat: Dry, rocky, thin soil on the south side of hilltops, dry mountain valleys and rocky ridges. Range: Eastern Washington to Nevada. East to Wyoming, Utah, and Colorado. Season: April — May.

127

Desert Evening Primrose, Caespitose Evening Primrose
Evening Primrose Family (*Onagraceae*)   *Oenothera caespitosa*

Name source: Greek. *Oenothera*—wine-scenting, given to plant used for that purpose; *caespitosa*—growing in tufts.

Description: Perennial. Acaulescent. Leaves oblanceolate, sinuate-dentate to subentire, blades 3-10 cm. Petioles equaling blades. Hypanthium 5-12 cm long, often reddish. Sepals 2.5-3.5 cm. Petals white, aging pink to red, broadly obcordate, 2.5-6.5 cm long. Stamens 8. Sepals 4, reflexed. Leaves and roots edible, but bitter.

Habitat: Talus slopes, roadcuts, and dry hills. Range: Over much of western United States. Season: May—July.

Pink Fairies, Deerhorn, Ragged Robin, Elkhorn Clarkia
Evening Primrose Family (*Onagraceae*)   *Clarkia pulchella*

Name source: *Clarkia* — for Captain William Clark of Lewis and Clark Expedition; *pulchella* — beauty.

Description: Annual with simple alternate linear obtuse leaves. Ovary inferior, calyx tube prolonged beyond it, lobes linear and reflexed. Four petals deeply 3-lobed, lavender to rose-purple, .5-2.5 mm long, a smaller pair of lobes at juncture of blade and claw. Anthers of fertile stamens strongly coiled. Capsules 4-sided, 1-2 cm long.

Habitat: Dry open ground. Range: Southern interior British Columbia to Oregon (east side of Cascades), California. East to western Montana and Utah. Season: Early to mid-July.

Desert Shooting Star, Bonneville Shooting Star
Primrose Family (*Primulaceae*)   *Dodecatheon conjugens*

Name source: Greek. *Dodeka* — 12, *theon* — gods (protected by the gods); *conjugens* — paired.

Description: Perennial, 1-3 dm tall. Leaves basal, obovate to oblong-oblanceolate, 3-20 cm long, several times as long as broad, entire. Flowers showy, 4-5 parts, corolla 1-3 cm, deep purple to rose-purple, rarely white tinged with yellow. Pistil 1.

Habitat: Seepages in sagebrush to mountain meadows. Range: East slopes of Cascades from British Columbia to northern California. East to Alberta and Wyoming. Season: March — June.

Pink Annual Phlox, Slender Phlox
Phlox Family (*Polemoniaceae*)   *Microsteris gracilis*

Name source: Greek. *Mikros*—small, *sterizo*—to support (supposed reference to small size of plant); *gracilis*—slender, gracefully slight in form.

Description: Annual, simple below branched above, to 2 dm tall. Leaves linear or lance-linear to elliptic, or the lower obovate, up to 5 cm long and 8 mm wide. Calyx 5-6 mm. Corolla 5-15 mm, with pink to purple lobes and yellow tube.

Habitat: Dry packed soil to moderately moist open places, mostly in foothills and lowlands. Range: Southern British Columbia to Montana; south to southern California and New Mexico. Season: May—August.

Needle-leaved Phlox
Phlox Family (*Polemoniaceae*)   *Phlox aculeata*

Name source: *Phlox*—direct transliteration of Greek *flame,* refers to brightly colored flowers; *aculeata*—with thorns, prickly, pointed.

Description: Perennial, compactly branched and tufted, 5-15 cm tall. Leaves firm, linear, 1-3.5 cm long, 0.5-1.5 mm wide. Corolla white to pink to blue, tube 10-15 mm long, lobes 3-12 mm long. While Phlox normally have 5 petals they have been known to have 4, 6, or on rare occasions, 7 petals. Phlox species are good garden plants.

Habitat: Dry, open, sometimes alkaline places, with sagebrush. Range: Eastern base of Cascades in Oregon to Idaho. Season: April—June.

Gray Phlox
Phlox Family (*Polemoniaceae*) *Phlox hoodii*

Name source: *Phlox* — direct transliteration of Greek word for flame.

Description: Perennial, forming compact low mat or cushion. Leaves firm, pungent, narrowly linear, 4-11 mm long and 0.5 mm wide. Corolla bluish or pink to white, tube 4-13 mm long, lobes 4-7 mm.

Habitat: Dry stony ground; open, rocky or sandy soil in foothills, valleys, plains. Commonly with sagebrush. Range: Eastern base of Cascades; Klickitat County, Washington to Modoc County, California. East to Montana, Wyoming, Utah, New Mexico. Season: April — July.

Annual Polemonium
Phlox Family (*Polemoniaceae*)   *Polemonium micranthum*

Name source: From *Polemon* — Greek philosopher, or *polemos* — strife, discovery of supposed
properties caused war between two kings; *micranthum* — small flowered.

Description: Slender, simple to more or less branched annual, 6-30 cm tall. Leaves alternate,
pinnate, 2-4 cm long; leaflets 7-11, thin, oblanceolate to narrowly elliptic, 2-9 mm long, and
1-4 mm wide. Flower small, white, 2-6 mm long, broadly campanulate. Uniqueness of annual
habit and small corolla and sympodial stems put it often into *Polemoniella* (monotypic genus).

Habitat: Open dry, or drying moist ground, plains, and foothills; often with sagebrush. Range:
Washington and southern British Columbia to California, Utah, western Montana. Chiefly
east of Cascades. Season: March—May.

Woolly-breeches, Pussyfoot, Dwarf Waterleaf
Waterleaf Family (*Hydrophyllaceae*)   *Hydrophyllum capitatum*

Name source: Greek. *Hydor* — water, *phyllon* — leaf; *capitatum* — head shaped.

Description: Perennial, 1-4.5 dm tall. Leaves few, large, long-petioled. Blade broadly ovate in outline, 5-15 cm long and 3-12 cm wide, pinnately divided or parted into 5-11 sessile leaflets or divisions, the upper confluent, the lower approximate or remote; leaflets acute to obtuse or rounded, with rounded entire margins or commonly some with 1 or 2 large entire-margined lobes. Calyx lobes 3-4 mm long. Corolla purplish blue to white, 5-9 mm long.

Habitat: Moist soil in sagebrush or conifer woods, and on damp, shady streambanks. Range: Southern British Columbia and Alberta to central California and Colorado. East of Cascade summit. Season: March — July.

Varied-leaf Phacelia, Virgate Phacelia
Waterleaf Family (*Hydrophyllaceae*)   *Phacelia heterophylla*

Name source: Greek. *Phakelos* — fascicle, referring to the congested inflorescence; *hetero-phylla* — leaves of several forms (varied).

Description: Biennial or short lived perennial, 2-12 dm tall, with a single erect stem or one surrounded by several smaller stems. Herbage gray or green. Leaves alternate, extensively variable, lower ones lanceolate to ovate, 5-15 cm long, pinnate (rarely entire), the terminal division longest. Upper cauline reduced, the topmost entire. 1-2 pistilets. 5-merous. Corolla 5-merous, dull white to purplish, 3-6 mm. Stamens showy, 8-10 mm long. Leaves may cause skin irritation.

Habitat: Damp ground, rocky open places or in pine woods. Range: Washington and adjacent southern British Columbia to central California, Arizona, New Mexico; east to Montana, Wyoming, Utah. Season: May — July.

Narrow-leaved Phacelia
Waterleaf Family (*Hydrophyllaceae*)   *Phacelia linearis*

Name source: Greek. *Phakelos* — a fascicle, referring to congested inflorescence; *linearis* — of uniform width.

Description: Erect annual 1-5 dm tall, simple or branched. Leaves all cauline, sessile or short-petioled, linear, 1.5-11 cm long, 1.5-12 mm wide, some with 1-4 divergent narrow segments below middle. Flowers crowded, calyx lobes narrow. Corolla blue to lavender to white, pelviform, very broadly campanulate, 6-10 mm long, 10-18 mm wide. Stamens about equaling corolla lobes. Common, showy plant. Leaves may cause skin irritation.

Habitat: Dry sandy or rocky soil, open places in foothills and plains. Range: British Columbia and Alberta to northern California, Utah, Wyoming. Chiefly east of Cascades. Season: April — June.

Bluebell, Long-flowered Lungwort
Borage Family (*Boraginaceae*)   *Mertensia longiflora*

Name source: *Mertensia*—for F.C. Mertens, 1764-1831, German botanist; *longiflora*—long flower.

Description: Perennial. 1 to occasionally 2 or 3 stems, 0.5-2.5 dm tall. Basal leaves rarely develop on flowering plants. Cauline leaves rather few, mostly sessile or nearly so, 2-8 cm long. Corolla 1-2.5 cm long, tube 2-3 times as long as the slightly expanded shallowly-lobed limb.

Habitat: Damp meadows, open or lightly shaded plains and foothills, often with sagebrush or Ponderosa Pine below 5,000 feet. Range: Southern British Columbia to central Oregon, east of Cascades and rarely, to northern California; east to northwestern Montana and Boise, Idaho. Season: April—June.

138

Forget-me-not, Yellow-and blue Scorpion Grass
Borage Family (*Boraginaceae*)   *Myosotis discolor*

Name source: Greek. *Mus* — mouse, *ous* — ear, referring to the leaf of some species; *discolor* — of different colors.

Description: Slender branching annual, 1-5 dm tall. Leaves 1-4 cm long, 2-8 mm wide, the basal often rosulate, lance-linear or the lower oblanceolate. Inflorescence of helicoid, false racemes. Calyx 5-lobed. Corolla salverform or broadly funnelform, pale yellow, changing to blue and violet, limb about 2 mm broad. Emblem of eternal love and friendship, woven into collars worn by knights of 14th century.

Habitat: Fields, waste places, and roadsides. Range: Naturalized from Europe. Washington to California; not as much east of Cascades in Oregon, mostly in Willamete and Umpqua Valleys. Season: April — August.

Index of Scientific Names

Index of Common Names